STRAIGHT FROM

THE LLAMA'S MOUTH

Eddie Watts

CONTENTS

INTRODUCTION

Imagine your favorite food. The one that disappears while you're "just tasting it."

That's this book.

Idioms are everywhere. We use them without thinking. But if you stop and really listen, they're bizarre. Who decided buttering someone up was a thing? And that elephant, why is he in a million rooms? And what, exactly, is in the pudding?

This book digs into the odd, hilarious, and sometimes baffling origins of the phrases we say every day. Some came from war.

Some from sports. A few from total accidents that just stuck around. Others, well, you'll find out soon enough.

Now grab the reins, hold onto your hat, and buckle up, buttercup.

Let's ride.

CHAPTER ONE

THE ANIMAL IN YOU

1. "You Can't Teach an Old Dog New Tricks"

The phrase means it's difficult to change someone's long-standing habits, especially as they get older. It first appeared in John Fitzherbert's *The Boke of Husbandry* (1534), where it referred to actual dog training: "The dogge must lerne when he is a whelpe, or els it will not be." By the 19th century it had become a universal metaphor for human stubbornness.

Fun Fact: Studies in neuroscience show that older brains can still develop new neural pathways. The phrase, it turns out, isn't entirely accurate.

2. "STRAIGHT FROM THE HORSE'S MOUTH"

Getting information "straight from the horse's mouth" means getting it directly from the most reliable source. The phrase comes from horse racing, where bettors checked a horse's teeth to determine its age and health, a more accurate method than relying on a jockey, trainer, or rumor. By the 1920s it had moved beyond racing into business, journalism, and everyday conversation.

Fun Fact: The phrase is closely related to "don't look a gift horse in the mouth," which also comes from judging a horse's value by its teeth.

3. "NOT MY CIRCUS, NOT MY MONKEYS"

The phrase means "this is not my problem." It comes from a Polish proverb, "Nie mój cyrk, nie moje małpy," traditionally used to signal staying out of unnecessary drama. It went global in the 21st century as a blunt, humorous way to decline involvement in someone else's mess.

Fun Fact: The phrase caught on particularly fast in customer service, which probably tells you something about customer service.

4. "LET THE CAT OUT OF THE BAG"

To "let the cat out of the bag" means to accidentally reveal a secret. One popular theory traces it to medieval markets, where dishonest merchants swapped a piglet for a cat in a sack. If the buyer opened the bag before paying, the scam was exposed. The phrase was first recorded in the 18th century.

Fun Fact: The same phrase exists in German: "die Katze aus dem Sack lassen," literally "let the cat out of the sack." Same scam, different language.

5. "Like a Bull in a China Shop"

To act "like a bull in a China shop" means to be clumsy or reckless in a delicate situation. The phrase appeared in the 19th century, though real bulls are often surprisingly careful in enclosed spaces. One theory links it to European marketplaces where cattle occasionally wandered into shops. Another connects it to circus acts where a bull's clumsiness was exaggerated for entertainment.

Fun Fact: In 2006, MythBusters tested this phrase by releasing real bulls into a China shop. Surprisingly, the bulls moved carefully and didn't break much, proving the idiom to be an exaggeration.

6. "A Wolf in Sheep's Clothing"

Someone who is "a wolf in sheep's clothing" appears harmless while actually being dangerous. The phrase comes from Aesop's Fables (6th century BC), where a wolf disguises itself in a sheepskin to infiltrate a flock. It later appeared in the Bible (Matthew 7:15), warning against false prophets. By the 16th century it was common shorthand for any kind of hidden threat.

Fun Fact: Psychologists and criminal profilers use it constantly, particularly for con artists and manipulative leaders.

7. "Let Sleeping Dogs Lie"

To "let sleeping dogs lie" means to leave a situation alone rather than risk stirring up trouble. The phrase comes from medieval hunting and guard dog training, where waking a sleeping dog could cause it to turn aggressive. It was first recorded in the 13th century in French and English proverbs, appeared in Chaucer's *Troilus and Criseyde* (1380), and later in Shakespeare, cementing the idea that reviving old conflicts rarely ends well.

Fun Fact: Lawyers and politicians know this one well. Reopening settled disputes rarely ends quietly.

8. "LIKE HERDING CATS"

To say something is "like herding cats" means trying to organize a chaotic, uncooperative group. The phrase showed up in the 1980s, rooted in the obvious fact that cats do not take direction. It spread quickly through business and management circles as shorthand for the specific frustration of getting people to cooperate. A 2000 Super Bowl commercial, in which cowboys attempted to herd cats across open range, pushed it fully into mainstream use.

Fun Fact: In tech culture, "cat herder" is a real informal title for project managers trying to keep unpredictable teams moving in the same direction.

9. "TILL THE COWS COME HOME"

To say something will happen "till the cows come home" means it will take a very long time, possibly forever. The phrase comes from rural Scotland and England, where cows were known to take their time returning from grazing, sometimes wandering for hours before slowly making their way back. First recorded in the late 16th century in Scottish literature and farming discussions, it became a metaphor for anything drawn-out: waiting for someone to stop talking, a project to finish, a situation to change.

Fun Fact: Groucho Marx put the phrase to good use: "I could dance with you till the cows come home. On second thought, I'd rather dance with the cows till you come home."

10. "When Pigs Fly"

To say "when pigs fly" means something is impossible and will never happen. The phrase comes from medieval European proverbs, where absurd imagery was used to mock unrealistic expectations. The first recorded version appeared in 1616 in John Withals' dictionary: "Pigs fly in the air with their tails forward." By the 19th century it had become the standard sarcastic dismissal for anything unlikely.

Fun Fact: Other languages have their own versions. In French, the equivalent is "when hens have teeth." In Spanish, "when frogs grow hair."

11. "A Little Bird Told Me"

To say "a little bird told me" means you learned something from a secret or unnamed source. The phrase has Biblical roots, appearing in Ecclesiastes 10:20, which warns that private thoughts may still be overheard: a bird of the air shall carry the voice. By the 18th and 19th centuries it was common shorthand for keeping a source anonymous, and it still turns up in journalism, gossip, and storytelling.

Fun Fact: Some historians believe the phrase may also connect to actual messenger pigeons, which carried secret communications during wartime.

12. "THE ELEPHANT IN THE ROOM"

To say there is "an elephant in the room" means there is an obvious problem everyone is avoiding. The phrase originated in 19th-century Russian fables, where a character notices small details but ignores a giant elephant standing right there, a pointed image for how people sidestep uncomfortable truths. It moved into English literature by the early 20th century and became standard in politics, business, and anywhere difficult conversations get quietly shelved.

Fun Fact: A 1959 New York Times article used the phrase to describe major unspoken political issues, helping push it further into mainstream use.

13. "CURIOSITY KILLED THE CAT"

The phrase serves as a warning against unnecessary risk or meddling. The original version, "care killed the cat," appeared in 16th-century English literature, where "care" meant worry or sorrow, not curiosity. By the 19th century the phrase had shifted to emphasize the dangers of prying. What rarely gets mentioned is the full proverb: "Curiosity killed the cat, but satisfaction brought it back."

Fun Fact: Cats are naturally inclined to squeeze into tight spaces and investigate risky situations. The phrase, at least, picked the right animal.

14. "THE LION'S SHARE"

To receive "the lion's share" means to get the largest portion of something. The phrase comes from Aesop's Fables (6th century BC), where a lion tricks other animals into hunting for him, then claims all the meat for himself. By the 18th and 19th centuries it was common in business, law, and literature to describe one party taking the biggest cut of profits or resources.

Fun Fact: Sports, finance, boardrooms. The biggest rewards go to whoever's running the table.

15. "LIKE A DEER IN HEADLIGHTS"

To be "like a deer in headlights" means to be so startled that you freeze and can't react. The phrase comes from real animal behavior: deer caught in vehicle headlights often stop instead of running, making them vulnerable. The idiom became widely used in the late 20th century to describe anyone who appears unprepared or unable to respond under pressure.

Fun Fact: Deer have a reflective layer in their eyes called the tapetum lucidum, which improves night vision but also causes their eyes to glow in the dark. Sudden bright light temporarily disorients them, which is why they hesitate.

16. "CRY WOLF"

To "cry wolf" means to raise false alarms so often that people stop believing you, even when you're telling the truth. The phrase comes from Aesop's "The Boy Who Cried Wolf," written around 600 BC. A bored shepherd repeatedly fakes a wolf attack for attention. When a real wolf arrives, nobody comes. The phrase became a standard warning about lying and exaggeration, particularly in news media, security, and personal relationships.

Fun Fact: False alarms erode trust. The lesson hasn't changed in 2,600 years.

17. "Monkey See, Monkey Do"

The phrase means copying someone's actions without thinking through the consequences. It comes from early 20th-century American slang, likely influenced by observations of monkeys mimicking human behavior. It first appeared in print in 1911, used to describe how children imitate adults. Over time it became shorthand for mindless imitation across fads, social behavior, and marketing.

Fun Fact: The phrase maps neatly onto internet culture, where viral challenges spread largely because people copy what they see without stopping to ask why.

18. "Dog-Eat-Dog World"

A "dog-eat-dog world" describes a ruthless, competitive environment where people will do anything to get ahead. The phrase actually inverts an older Latin proverb, "Canis caninam non est," meaning a dog does not eat another dog, which implied mutual respect. By the 18th and 19th centuries the meaning had flipped completely, becoming shorthand for aggressive competition and harsh survival dynamics.

Fun Fact: The phrase gets linked regularly to Darwinian theory, framing cutthroat competition as simple survival of the fittest.

19. "A Kangaroo Court"

A "kangaroo court" is an unofficial, biased, or corrupt proceeding where the verdict is predetermined. The phrase appeared in 19th-century America, likely describing the hasty, arbitrary justice of frontier towns. One theory connects it to Australian gold rush miners who held informal trials that consistently favored landowners. The word "kangaroo" may refer to how quickly these courts jumped to conclusions.

Fun Fact: The phrase saw heavy use during World War II to describe show trials in totalitarian regimes, where guilty verdicts were decided before proceedings began.

20. "A Leopard Can't Change Its Spots"

The phrase means people cannot change their true nature. It comes from the Bible, Jeremiah 13:23, which asks whether a leopard can change its spots in the same breath as asking whether someone accustomed to evil can learn to do good. By the 16th and 17th centuries it had settled into English proverbs as shorthand for the idea that deep habits don't shift.

Fun Fact: Modern psychology suggests people actually can change with sustained effort and motivation. The leopard, it turns out, may have options.

CHAPTER TWO

WHO'S HUNGRY?

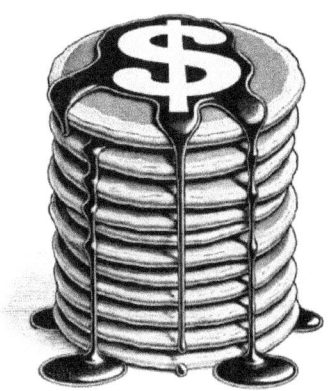

1. "SELL LIKE HOTCAKES"

To say something "sells like hotcakes" means it is extremely popular and moves fast. The phrase comes from the early 19th century, when hotcakes (another word for pancakes) were a staple at fairs, church events, and markets. Cheap, easy to make in bulk, and served quickly, they sold out reliably, which turned them into a metaphor for anything that becomes an instant hit. It landed in marketing and business and never left.

Fun Fact: French has a direct equivalent: "se vendre comme des petits pains," meaning to sell like little breads.

2. "USE YOUR NOODLE"

To "use your noodle" means to think carefully or apply some intel-ligence to a problem. The phrase comes from early 20th-century American slang, where "noodle" was a casual term for head or brain. One theory ties it to Italian immigrants, where "nudel" (pasta) was jokingly applied to someone's head, pasta and brains sharing a certain textural resemblance. By the mid-1900s, teachers and bosses were saying it constantly.

Fun Fact: French has a similar construction: "se creuser la tête," meaning to dig into one's head.

3. "AS USEFUL AS A CHOCOLATE TEAPOT"

To say something is "as useful as a chocolate teapot" means it is completely impractical. The phrase comes from 20th-century British English, where it described things that serve no real func-tion. A teapot made of chocolate would melt the moment hot tea hit it. The phrase gets applied to pointless inventions, unhelpful advice, and unreliable people.

Fun Fact: In 2008, scientists at Nestlé built a real chocolate teapot that survived long enough to pour a cup of tea. It was still not particularly useful.

4. "TAKE IT WITH A GRAIN OF SALT"

To "take something with a grain of salt" means to be skeptical and not fully accept what you hear. The phrase traces to Pliny the Elder's *Natural History* (77 AD), where a pinch of salt was included in a possible antidote to poison, suggesting that a small measure of skepticism could neutralize bad information. By the 17th and 18th centuries it was common advice against accepting claims at face value, particularly in politics and gossip.

Fun Fact: In many cultures, spilling salt is bad luck. Throwing a pinch over your shoulder is said to ward off whatever followed the spill.

5. "SPILL THE BEANS"

To "spill the beans" means to reveal a secret, often by accident. One popular theory traces it to ancient Greece, where elections were sometimes held using beans: white for yes, black for no. If someone knocked over the container before the count was done, the result was exposed early. The phrase appeared in American newspapers in the early 20th century and became standard short-hand for letting something slip.

Fun Fact: Spanish has a similar idea: "irse de la lengua," meaning to let your tongue run away with you.

6. "BRING HOME THE BACON"

To "bring home the bacon" means to earn money and support yourself or your family. The phrase traces to medieval England, where a church in Dunmow, Essex, awarded a side of bacon to married couples who could prove they had lived in harmony for a full year. It later picked up additional momentum in early 20th-century American boxing, where prizefighters were urged to win the fight and bring home the earnings. The two uses merged. The meaning stuck.

Fun Fact: The Dunmow Flitch of Bacon tradition still exists. Couples still compete to prove their happiness and walk away with a ceremonial side of bacon.

7. "CHEW THE FAT"

To "chew the fat" means to have a long, casual conversation in a relaxed setting. The phrase is believed to come from sailors and soldiers in the 16th and 17th centuries, who chewed on tough salted meat while passing time together. By the 19th century it had become a metaphor for unhurried conversation, particularly in working-class communities.

Fun Fact: In parts of Scotland, the equivalent is "having a blether," and the tradition of sharing fatty meats while exchanging news was considered a basic act of hospitality.

8. "PIECE OF CAKE"

To say something is a "piece of cake" means it requires almost no effort. The phrase likely comes from 19th and early 20th-century cakewalks, where participants competed in a walking contest and the winner received a cake as a prize. Since the contest was considered light and fun, it became a metaphor for anything easy. British pilots in World War II used it for easy missions. It fit.

Fun Fact: Spanish has "pan comido," meaning eaten bread. German has "ein Kinderspiel," a child's game. Same idea, different snacks.

9. "EAT HUMBLE PIE"

To "eat humble pie" means to admit a mistake and accept the humiliation that comes with it. In the Middle Ages, after a hunt, the lord of the manor ate the best cuts while lower-ranking people got a dish called "umble pie," made from the less desirable parts: liver, intestines, heart. The dish carried a clear social stigma. By the 17th century, "umble" and "humble" had blurred together due to similar pronunciation, and eating it became a metaphor for public embarrassment.

Fun Fact: Some modern chefs recreate humble pie using offal-based fillings as a nod to the medieval original. It remains an acquired taste.

10. "OUT OF THE FRYING PAN AND INTO THE FIRE"

When someone escapes one bad situation only to land in a worse one, they've gone "out of the frying pan into the fire." The phrase appears in John Heywood's 1546 proverb collection, making it one of the oldest idioms still in common use. The image is straightforward: a fish escaping a hot pan lands directly in the fire beneath it. The phrase appeared in Edmund Spenser's *The Faerie Queene* (1590) and Cervantes' *Don Quixote* (1615), and it has not left.

Fun Fact: Italian has a version that goes from frying pan to embers. German goes from rain to river. The specifics change. The bad luck doesn't.

11. "GO BANANAS"

To "go bananas" means to act crazy, get wildly excited, or completely lose control. The phrase came out of American slang in the mid-20th century, likely inspired by the unpredictable behavior of monkeys around bananas. It caught on in the 1950s and 1960s in sports and entertainment, and expanded over time to cover losing one's temper as well.

Fun Fact: "Go ape" was popular in the same era for the same reasons. Apparently mid-century Americans found primates a reliable benchmark for chaos.

12. "Too Many Cooks Spoil the Broth"

The phrase means that when too many people get involved in something, their conflicting input ruins it rather than improves it. It comes from medieval European kitchens, where multiple cooks working the same dish reliably produced disaster. The phrase was first recorded in the 16th century in English and German proverbs. Every century finds a new application.

Fun Fact: A Chinese equivalent translates roughly to "three monks have no water to drink." Too many people responsible means nobody is.

13. "Like Two Peas in a Pod"

To say two people are "like two peas in a pod" means they are nearly identical in personality, appearance, or behavior. The phrase comes from the way peas actually grow: uniform in shape, packed tightly together. It was first recorded in John Lyly's *Euphues and His England* (1580): "Wherin I am like two peason in one podde." By the 19th and 20th centuries it had become standard shorthand for close friendships, twins, and couples who seem cut from the same cloth.

Fun Fact: Spanish has "parecerse como dos gotas de agua," meaning to resemble each other like two drops of water. Same idea, no vegetables involved.

14. "Eat Someone Alive"

To "eat someone alive" means to aggressively dominate, criticize, or defeat someone completely. The phrase draws on the natural image of a predator consuming prey, and first appeared in the 19th century in political and legal contexts, where a powerful speaker could systematically dismantle an opponent in debate. It spread into sports, business, and everyday use from there.

Fun Fact: The phrase tends to come up in negotiations and competitive sport, where "alive" does a lot of work as a qualifier. Being eaten the other way is presumably worse.

15. "In a Pickle"

To be "in a pickle" means to be stuck in a difficult or messy situation. The phrase dates to the 16th century, with one of its earliest appearances in Shakespeare's *The Tempest* (1611): "How camest thou in this pickle?" It likely comes from Dutch and English pickling traditions, where preserved ingredients became impossible to separate once combined. Trapped, with no clean way out. The image held.

Fun Fact: In baseball, a pickle is when a runner gets caught between two bases while fielders close in from both sides. Stuck, with no good option. The metaphor holds.

16. "Butter Someone Up"

To "butter someone up" means to flatter someone excessively to gain their favor. The phrase has roots in ancient Indian religious rituals, where butter (ghee) was smeared on statues as an act of devotion, hoping for blessings in return. By the 16th and 17th centuries it had appeared in English literature as a metaphor for excessive praise, the idea being that flattery smooths people over the same way butter smooths food.

Fun Fact: "Buttering up the boss" became its own subcategory of the phrase, specific enough to describe a whole workplace dynamic.

17. "FULL OF BEANS"

To be "full of beans" means to be energetic, enthusiastic, and hard to slow down. The phrase dates to the 19th century, when horses and livestock were fed beans before races or heavy labor to boost their energy. It crossed over to people as a description for anyone unusually animated or high-spirited.

Fun Fact: The phrase originally carried a second meaning: someone full of nonsense rather than energy. Which is why "full of beans" can still occasionally mean "not to be taken seriously," depending on who's saying it.

18. "EGG ON YOUR FACE"

To have "egg on your face" means to be visibly embarrassed by something you did or said. One theory traces it to audiences throwing eggs at poor performers, leaving them literally marked. Another points to sloppy eating, where smeared egg became a source of ridicule. Either way, the image stuck.

Fun Fact: In the early 20th century, eggs weren't always cheap or easy to come by, so having one on your face carried a secondary implication: you could afford to waste food, and you still managed to look foolish.

19. "NOT MY CUP OF TEA"

To say something is "not my cup of tea" means it simply isn't to your liking. The phrase comes from British tea culture, where selecting a blend was a personal and considered choice. Declining one politely became its own expression. It first appeared in British literature in the early 20th century, initially as a positive: "my cup of tea" meant something enjoyable. By the 1930s the negative version had taken over.

Fun Fact: The phrase remains more common in British English. Americans tend to say "not my thing," which is less interesting but faster.

20. "SALT OF THE EARTH"

To call someone the "salt of the earth" means they are genuinely good, honest, and dependable. The phrase comes from the Bible, Matthew 5:13, where Jesus tells his followers they are the salt of the earth and asks what happens when salt loses its flavor. In ancient times, salt was extraordinarily valuable: used for preserving food, traded as currency, and offered in religious ceremonies. The compliment carried real weight.

Fun Fact: The word "salary" comes from the Latin "salarium," meaning payment in salt. The phrase picked a good metaphor.

CHAPTER THREE

WE ARE THE WAY WE ARE

1. "MAD AS A HATTER"

To be "mad as a hatter" means to be completely unhinged. The phrase comes from 19th-century England, where hat makers were regularly poisoned by mercury used in the felting process. Prolonged exposure caused tremors, hallucinations, and erratic behavior, a condition that became known as Mad Hatter's disease. The phrase got its most famous airing in Lewis Carroll's *Alice's Adventures in Wonderland* (1865).

Fun Fact: Carroll's Mad Hatter wasn't actually based on mercury poisoning. Carroll just liked strange characters. The historical connection arrived later and made the whole thing feel more intentional than it was.

2. "By the Skin of Your Teeth"

To escape "by the skin of your teeth" means to barely make it through. The phrase comes from the Bible, Job 19:20: "I am escaped with the skin of my teeth." Since teeth don't have skin, scholars believe the phrase was deliberately paradoxical, describing something impossibly thin as a way of emphasizing how little margin there was. By the 17th century it was standard shorthand for any narrow escape.

Fun Fact: Several languages use "by a hair's width" for the same idea. The specifics vary. The feeling of almost not making it is universal.

3. "Have a Chip on Your Shoulder"

To "have a chip on your shoulder" means to carry resentment or be itching for a fight over past grievances. The phrase comes from 19th-century America, where young men literally balanced a small wooden chip on their shoulder and dared others to knock it off. An 1830 newspaper article described boys in New York doing exactly this as a way to signal their readiness to brawl. Over time it became a metaphor for anyone who walks around defensive and looking for an excuse.

Fun Fact: "Carrying a monkey on your back" covers similar territory in some cultures, though it leans more toward being weighed down by an unresolved problem than looking for a fight.

4. "Bite the Bullet"

To "bite the bullet" means to endure something painful or difficult without flinching. The phrase comes from battlefield medicine in the 19th century, when wounded soldiers bit down on a bullet during surgery before anesthesia was available. Some historians push the origin back to the 18th century, when soldiers bit musket bullets to keep still during battle. Either way, the image is the same: pain you have to get through.

Fun Fact: It wasn't always bullets. Historical records show wooden sticks and leather straps were also common. Bullets were just more memorable.

5. "Pull Someone's Leg"

To "pull someone's leg" means to tease or trick someone in a playful way. The origins are genuinely debated. One theory connects it to 18th-century London thieves who tripped victims by grabbing their legs before robbing them, though that meaning faded quickly. By the early 20th century the phrase had fully converted to lighthearted territory, particularly in British and American humor where teasing tends to double as affection.

Fun Fact: "Taking someone for a ride" covers similar ground in some cultures, though it implies a longer con and a less friendly intent.

6. "Give Someone the Cold Shoulder"

To "give someone the cold shoulder" means to deliberately ignore or exclude someone. The phrase comes from medieval England, where hosts would serve a cold shoulder of mutton to unwelcome guests as a pointed hint to leave. It appeared in print in the early 19th century, notably in Sir Walter Scott's novels, as shorthand for deliberate indifference.

Fun Fact: In some cultures, a shoulder cut of meat is actually a mark of hospitality. The phrase traveled in the opposite direction entirely.

7. "SEE EYE TO EYE"

To "see eye to eye" means to be in complete agreement. The phrase comes from the Bible, Isaiah 52:8, where it described unity and shared vision. By the 19th century it had moved into everyday use for mutual understanding in business, relationships, and diplomacy.

Fun Fact: Body language research consistently links direct eye contact with honesty and agreement, which means the idiom accidentally got the science right.

8. "DON'T DRINK THE KOOL-AID"

To "drink the Kool-Aid" means to follow a belief or leader without questioning it. The phrase comes from the 1978 Jonestown Massacre, where cult leader Jim Jones ordered his followers to drink cyanide-laced Flavor Aid. The drink was widely misidentified as Kool-Aid, and the name stuck. By the 1980s it had become a metaphor for blind loyalty and groupthink, used in politics, business, and social movements.

Fun Fact: The drink used at Jonestown was actually Flavor Aid, not Kool-Aid. Kool-Aid got the association anyway and has since made occasional lighthearted references to it in marketing. Flavor Aid, the actual brand involved, remains largely unknown.

9. "A Sight for Sore Eyes"

To call something "a sight for sore eyes" means it is a welcome and relieving thing to see, usually after a long absence or difficult stretch. The phrase was first recorded in 1738 in a letter by Jonathan Swift: "The sight of you is good for sore eyes." It has stayed close to its original meaning ever since.

Fun Fact: Some cultures use "balm for the eyes" instead, which lands slightly more poetic and slightly less medical.

10. "Keep Your Finger on the Pulse"

To "keep your finger on the pulse" means to stay informed about what's changing in a given situation. The phrase comes directly from medicine, where checking a patient's pulse allows a doctor to monitor their condition and respond quickly. It moved into metaphorical use in the 19th century, particularly in politics, journalism, and business.

Fun Fact: Some historians trace the phrase back to ancient Greek medicine, where physicians used pulse diagnosis as a primary diagnostic tool long before modern instruments existed.

11. "Wear Your Heart on Your Sleeve"

To "wear your heart on your sleeve" means to openly show your emotions rather than hide them. The phrase dates to medieval jousting tournaments, where knights wore the colors or tokens of their beloved on their sleeves as a public declaration. Shakespeare used it in *Othello* (1604), where Iago says he will wear his heart upon his sleeve "for daws to peck at." By the 19th century it had settled into a general metaphor for emotional openness.

Fun Fact: In modern psychology, people who wear their heart on their sleeve are described as emotionally expressive and easy to read, which is either a compliment or a liability depending on the situation.

12. "BLOOD, SWEAT, AND TEARS"

The phrase describes extreme effort and sacrifice. It became famous through Winston Churchill's 1940 speech: "I have nothing to offer but blood, toil, tears, and sweat." But the combination has Biblical roots in Luke 22:44, describing Jesus sweating great drops of blood before the crucifixion, and it appeared in military writing long before Churchill picked it up.

Fun Fact: The phrase gave the rock band Blood, Sweat and Tears their name. They had a good run in the late 1960s and 70s, which is more than most phrases can claim.

13. "BREAK A LEG"

To "break a leg" means good luck, particularly in theater, where saying "good luck" directly was considered bad luck. The work-around was an ironic alternative that couldn't jinx anything. The superstition traces to 19th and early 20th-century performers. A second theory connects the phrase to "breaking" the leg in a deep bow or curtsy, the gesture a performer made after a successful show.

Fun Fact: Germany uses "Hals und Beinbruch," meaning neck and leg break. Italy goes with "In bocca al lupo," into the wolf's mouth. Theater people across cultures seem to agree that wishing someone well directly is asking for trouble.

14. "Green-Eyed Monster"

The "green-eyed monster" is jealousy. Shakespeare coined the phrase in *Othello* (1603), where Iago warns: "O, beware, my lord, of jealousy! It is the green-eyed monster which doth mock the meat it feeds on." He had already used green as a symbol of envy in *The Merchant of Venice* (1596). The color connection may come from ancient beliefs that strong emotions affected bile production, giving the envious a greenish cast.

Fun Fact: Psychologists and writers keep coming back to it for the same reason: jealousy tends to consume the person feeling it more than whoever it's aimed at.

15. "Head Over Heels"

The original phrase was "heels over head," which described a literal somersault and actually made spatial sense. By the 18th century it had flipped to "head over heels" while still referring to physical tumbling. The shift to romantic meaning happened in early 19th-century American English, where newspapers began using it to describe falling madly in love, and it never looked back.

Fun Fact: The phrase started as a description of falling down and became a description of falling in love. The overlap is not a coincidence. Many languages use some version of "falling" for romance, which suggests the feeling is pretty consistent across cultures.

16. "By a Hair's Breadth"

The phrase comes from the literal width of a human hair, roughly 70 microns across. English writers in the 1500s began using "a hair's breadth" to describe very small distances, and it appears in William Tyndale's 1526 Bible translation. By the 17th century it had expanded beyond measurement to describe any narrow escape or close call.

Fun Fact: A hair's breadth isn't even a fixed measurement. Blonde hair averages 0.05 mm. Black hair can reach 0.12 mm. The margin varies depending on whose hair you're measuring.

17. "GO FOR THE JUGULAR"

To "go for the jugular" means to attack an opponent's greatest weakness with full force. The phrase comes from predatory behavior: big cats and wolves instinctively target the jugular vein to bring down prey quickly. Hunters and naturalists picked up the language, and by the late 1800s it had moved into sports and politics as a description for decisive, aggressive strategy.

Fun Fact: Lions and tigers clamp the jugular with their canine teeth, causing loss of consciousness in seconds. Domestic cats do the same thing with mice. The instinct scaled up fine as a metaphor.

18. "BITE THE HAND THAT FEEDS YOU"

To "bite the hand that feeds you" means to turn against someone who supports or helps you. The idea is ancient, but the first recorded version appeared in 1732, when Henry Fielding used a variation in *The History of the Life of the Late Mr. Jonathan Wild the Great*, comparing an ungrateful person to a dog biting its owner. By the 1800s it was standard in politics, business, and personal relationships as a warning against betraying allies.

Fun Fact: Dogs aren't the worst offenders here. Parrots regularly nip their owners after being given treats, apparently as a dominance move. The hand that feeds them is the first target.

19. "Blood is Thicker Than Water"

The phrase means family bonds outlast any other relationship. It dates to at least the 1100s, with the earliest English version appearing in John Ray's 1670 proverb collection. Some historians argue the original meaning was actually reversed: "the blood of the covenant is thicker than the water of the womb," suggesting chosen bonds could matter more than family. The shorter, modern version won out by the 19th century.

Fun Fact: Human blood is only about three to four times more viscous than water. Nowhere near as dramatically thick as the phrase implies, but "moderately more viscous than water" never caught on as an idiom.

20. "A Bitter Pill to Swallow"

To have "a bitter pill to swallow" means to accept something unpleasant but necessary. The phrase comes from the 1700s, when medicine was literally a bitter pill: crushed herbs, opium, or mercury, difficult to get down but required for survival. It moved from medical literature into everyday speech by the 1800s as a metaphor for any hard truth that has to be accepted.

Fun Fact: Quinine, used to treat malaria, was so unbearably bitter that people started mixing it with gin to get it down. That's where the gin and tonic came from. Medicine has produced worse side effects.

CHAPTER FOUR

READ IT, SCREEN
IT, STREAM IT

1. "OPEN SESAME"

"Open Sesame" is a magical command that opens locked doors. It comes from the Arabian Nights tale *Ali Baba and the Forty Thieves*, where Ali Baba overhears thieves using the phrase to open a treasure cave. Scholars believe "sesame" was chosen because sesame seeds pop open when they ripen, a natural image for something unlocking effortlessly. The phrase became shorthand for easy access to anything guarded or hidden.

Fun Fact: A story from the Arabian Nights is still doing conceptual work in cybersecurity. Not bad for a talking cave.

2. "CATCH-22"

A "Catch-22" describes a situation where contradictory rules make it impossible to win. The phrase comes from Joseph Heller's 1961 novel of the same name. In the book, a U.S. Air Force pilot wants to stop flying dangerous missions by claiming insanity. The rule: wanting to avoid flying proves you're sane enough to recognize the danger, which means you have to keep flying. No exit.

Fun Fact: The novel originally used Catch-18, but the number was changed to avoid confusion with Leon Uris' *Mila 18*. A small editorial decision turned into one of the most used phrases in the English language.

3. "BURN THE MIDNIGHT OIL"

To "burn the midnight oil" means to stay up late working or studying. The phrase dates to the 1600s, when oil lamps were the only light source after dark, meaning late work literally cost you lamp oil. It appeared in Francis Quarles' *Emblemes* (1635): "Wee spend our mid-day sweat, our midnight oyle."

Fun Fact: Before electricity, late-night work was done by whale oil or tallow candle. It was expensive, it smelled, and it still had to get done.

4. "JUMP THE SHARK"

To "jump the shark" means something has passed its peak and is now in obvious decline. The phrase comes from a 1977 episode of *Happy Days* in which Fonzie literally jumps over a shark on water skis, a moment many viewers took as the show losing its grip on reality. The phrase spread in the 1990s and 2000s as shorthand for any TV series introducing desperate gimmicks to stay relevant, and eventually expanded to cover anything past its prime.

Fun Fact: The term was coined by pop culture writer Jon Hein, who later sold JumpTheShark.com to *TV Guide*. An idiom about decline turned into a transaction. Fonzie would probably approve.

5. "Down the Rabbit Hole"

To "go down the rabbit hole" means to get pulled into something strange, complex, or consuming, going deeper the further you go. The phrase comes from Lewis Carroll's *Alice's Adventures in Wonderland* (1865), where Alice falls into a rabbit hole and lands in a world that follows no recognizable rules. In modern use it maps almost perfectly onto internet browsing, where one link leads to another until you've lost an hour to something you never meant to read.

Fun Fact: Lewis Carroll first told the story verbally to a ten-year-old girl named Alice Liddell during a boat trip on July 4, 1862. She liked it enough to ask him to write it down. The rabbit hole started as something to keep a child entertained on the water.

6. "Holy Grail"

The "Holy Grail" means something highly sought after and nearly impossible to obtain. It comes from Arthurian legend, where the Holy Grail was the sacred cup used by Jesus at the Last Supper, pursued by knights as the ultimate divine relic. The phrase crossed into everyday use as a metaphor for any breakthrough, discovery, or achievement that feels just out of reach.

Fun Fact: The Grail has had a busy film career, most notably in *Indiana Jones and the Last Crusade* (1989) and *Monty Python and the*

Holy Grail (1975), which approached the subject with different levels of reverence.

7. "DR. JEKYLL AND MR. HYDE"

To call someone a "Dr. Jekyll and Mr. Hyde" means they have two completely opposite sides: one respectable, one dangerous. The phrase comes from Robert Louis Stevenson's 1886 novel *Strange Case of Dr. Jekyll and Mr. Hyde*, where a scientist's potion transforms him into his worst self. The novel explored the idea of hidden evil beneath a civilized surface, and the phrase became standard shorthand for anyone whose behavior shifts dramatically depending on the situation.

Fun Fact: The novel sparked early conversations about what would later be classified as dissociative identity disorder. Stevenson wrote the first draft in three to six days, reportedly in a fever dream. Some things write themselves.

8. "READ BETWEEN THE LINES"

To "read between the lines" means to find the meaning that isn't stated directly. The phrase comes from actual practice: during wartime and espionage, secret messages were written between the lines of ordinary letters using invisible ink, hiding communication in plain sight. By the 19th century the phrase had become a general metaphor for interpreting what someone really means beneath what they actually say.

Fun Fact: Hiding messages within normal-looking text is called steganography. It predates digital encryption by centuries and is still used in cybersecurity today.

9. "PANDORA'S BOX"

To "open Pandora's box" means to trigger a chain of unexpected and uncontrollable problems. The phrase comes from Greek mythology, where Pandora, the first woman, was given a jar by the gods and told not to open it. She did. Everything bad in the world came out, leaving only hope behind. By the 19th century the phrase was in wide use in literature and politics for any decision that produces consequences nobody anticipated.

Fun Fact: The original Greek word was "pithos," meaning jar. A translation error by Erasmus in the 16th century turned it into a box. The mistake has outlasted the original by five centuries.

10. "THE GAME IS AFOOT"

"The game is afoot" signals that something significant or exciting has begun. Shakespeare used a version of it in *King Henry IV, Part 1* (1597), but the phrase became famous through Arthur Conan Doyle's Sherlock Holmes, who used it to announce the start of an investigation. Holmes borrowed it from Shakespeare and made it his own so thoroughly that most people forget where it started.

Fun Fact: The phrase has been referenced across films, television, and video games for over a century. Holmes used it first in print. Everyone else has been catching up since.

11. "THE BEST-LAID PLANS"

The phrase means that even the most carefully prepared strategies can fall apart. It comes from Robert Burns' 1785 poem "To a Mouse": "The best-laid schemes o' mice an' men / Gang aft agley," which translates roughly to "often go awry." The phrase moved into common English use as a reminder that planning only goes so far.

Fun Fact: John Steinbeck took the title *Of Mice and Men* (1937) directly from Burns' poem. The theme followed the title.

12. "MOBY-DICK COMPLEX"

A "Moby-Dick complex" describes an obsessive, self-destructive pursuit of something unattainable. The phrase comes from Herman Melville's *Moby-Dick* (1851), where Captain Ahab's fixation on hunting the white whale consumes and ultimately destroys him. The term gets applied in psychology, business, and literature to anyone who chases an objective so relentlessly they stop accounting for the cost.

Fun Fact: Ahab was partially based on real whalers, including George Pollard Jr., whose ship was actually sunk by a sperm whale. Melville didn't have to stretch far.

13. "DORIAN GRAY SYNDROME"

A "Dorian Gray Syndrome" describes an obsession with youth, often at the expense of everything else. It comes from Oscar Wilde's *The Picture of Dorian Gray* (1890), where Dorian stays eternally young while a hidden portrait absorbs his moral decay. The phrase is used in psychology and popular culture for people consumed by anti-aging, appearance, or a refusal to grow up.

Fun Fact: "Dorian Gray Syndrome" is a recognized term in medical psychology, used to describe severe anxiety about aging and self-image. Wilde would have found that either flattering or appalling.

14. "THE RED SHIRT"

A "red shirt" is a character who is doomed from the start. The term comes from the original *Star Trek* series (1966-1969), where security officers in red uniforms died at a disproportionate rate on away missions. An unnamed crew member in a red shirt beaming down to a dangerous planet was essentially a signal to the audience. The term became pop culture shorthand for any expendable character introduced only to be killed off.

Fun Fact: Fans ran the numbers and confirmed red-shirted crew members had the highest fatality rate in the series. For the record, Captain Kirk wore gold, not red. He survived every episode regardless.

15. "YADA, YADA, YADA"

To say "yada, yada, yada" means to skip the unnecessary details. The phrase became a cultural fixture after a 1997 *Seinfeld* episode where characters used it to gloss over key parts of a story. But the phrase predates the show, believed to come from Yiddish-American communities where similar words indicated meaningless or excessive chatter.

Fun Fact: *Seinfeld* didn't coin the phrase, but after the episode aired it was added to the Oxford English Dictionary. The show got the credit anyway. Yada, yada, yada.

16. "THE PEN IS MIGHTIER THAN THE SWORD"

The phrase means that words and ideas create more lasting change than force. It was coined by Edward Bulwer-Lytton in his 1839 play *Richelieu*: "Beneath the rule of men entirely great, the pen is mightier than the sword." The idea itself is older, running through ancient philosophy, religious texts, and political writing that favored persuasion over war.

Fun Fact: The phrase has been used so widely in politics, journalism, and activism that it has become its own argument for itself.

17. "THE BUTLER DID IT"

"The butler did it" is shorthand for a mystery plot twist where the least suspicious character turns out to be the killer. Butlers appeared in early detective fiction as loyal, discreet, and therefore useful suspects. The phrase is often attributed to Mary Roberts Rinehart, whose 1930 novel *The Door* features a killer butler, though she never used that exact wording. The trope became so familiar it was parodied almost as often as it was used sincerely.

Fun Fact: Agatha Christie avoided the guilty butler deliberately, considering it too obvious. When the queen of mystery thinks a twist is overdone, it's overdone.

18. "DEUS EX MACHINA"

"Deus ex machina," Latin for "god from the machine," describes a sudden, improbable event that resolves a story's central problem. It comes from ancient Greek theater, where a mechanical crane lowered an actor playing a god onto the stage to fix everything neatly. Once considered a valid dramatic device, it now reads as a storytelling shortcut, the narrative equivalent of giving up.

Fun Fact: The giant eagles arriving to rescue Frodo and Sam at the end of *The Lord of the Rings: The Return of the King* (2003) is one of the most debated examples in modern film. Tolkien fans have been arguing about whether it counts ever since.

19. "We're Gonna Need a Bigger Boat"

The phrase signals that a situation is far more serious than anyone prepared for. It comes from *Jaws* (1975), when Chief Brody gets his first close look at the shark and tells the captain they're going to need a bigger boat. The line was improvised by Roy Scheider. It became one of the most quoted lines in movie history and now gets used any time resources or preparation fall obviously short.

Fun Fact: The line has been referenced in *The Simpsons*, *Sharknado*, and dozens of other productions. An improvised moment of panic turned into a permanent entry in the cultural vocabulary.

20. "Chekhov's Gun"

"Chekhov's gun" is a storytelling principle: if something is introduced early, it must matter later. Anton Chekhov put it plainly: "If you say in the first chapter that there is a rifle hanging on the wall, in the second or third chapter it absolutely must go off." The concept pushes writers toward purposeful storytelling, where nothing appears without earning its place.

Fun Fact: *Die Hard* (1988) uses it cleanly: John McClane's habit of going barefoot, established early, becomes a serious liability when he's forced to walk across broken glass. Small detail, large consequences. Chekhov approved, presumably.

"BUT WHAT ABOUT THE LLAMAS?"

So, you're half-way through the book and you've learned a ton about idioms, and yet… there's still an elephant in the room. Or rather, a llama. Why was this book called *Straight from the Llama's Mouth*? Do llamas even have anything to do with idioms? Not really. But since we dragged llamas into this, it only seems fair to give them a moment.

Llamas hum when they're content, which is adorable. They're fluffy, four-legged kazoos. Scientists aren't sure why they do it, but I like to think they're just vibing to their own personal soundtrack.

When annoyed, llamas make weird gargling noises that sound like a mix between a drain clogging and a disgruntled goose. If you hear this noise, it's best to back away slowly, or risk a face full of llama spit.

The Incas used llamas as messengers, which sounds impressive until you realize llamas are not great at following directions and have a deep-rooted passion for taking snack breaks. Imagine sending an urgent message, only for your llama to stop and chew on some grass for three hours.

In 2015, two llamas became internet sensations after escaping from an assisted living facility in Arizona, where they were visiting as therapy animals. The daring duo then led authorities on a low-speed, high-drama chase for nearly three hours, dodging lasso-wielding humans and delighting the internet in the process. In the end, both llamas were safely captured. No harm, just legendary status.

There's your llama trivia. They earned it.

CHAPTER FIVE

THE SPORTS COLUMN

1. "Throw Your Hat in the Ring"

To "throw your hat in the ring" means to officially enter a competition. The phrase comes from 19th-century boxing, where a challenger literally tossed their hat into the ring to signal they wanted to fight. It moved into American politics in the early 1900s as shorthand for announcing a candidacy, and has since expanded to any competitive situation.

Fun Fact: Theodore Roosevelt made the phrase famous in 1912 when he announced his campaign for a third presidential term with "My hat's in the ring." The hat did not help.

2. "MOVE THE GOALPOSTS"

To "move the goalposts" means to change the rules or expectations unfairly, making success harder to reach. It comes from soccer and American football, where literally moving the goalposts mid-game would make scoring impossible. The phrase spread into business and politics in the 20th century as a description for shifting standards to keep someone from winning.

Fun Fact: Early soccer goalposts had no crossbar, meaning a ball kicked at any height counted as a goal. The crossbar wasn't standardized until 1863. The goalposts were, in a sense, always moveable.

3. "DARK HORSE"

A "dark horse" is an unexpected competitor who outperforms what anyone predicted. The phrase comes from horse racing, where an unknown horse suddenly beating the field left gamblers scrambling. Benjamin Disraeli used it in his 1831 novel *The Young Duke*, and by the late 19th century it had moved into politics to describe surprise candidates, then into sports, business, and entertainment.

Fun Fact: The most dramatic dark horse win in Kentucky Derby history was Donerail in 1913 at 91-1 odds. A two-dollar bet paid out $184.

4. "SAVED BY THE BELL"

The phrase comes from boxing, not burial. In early prizefighting, a boxer being overwhelmed near collapse could be rescued by the end-of-round bell before taking a knockout. The phrase appeared in newspapers by the 1890s in exactly this context. The story about Victorian coffins fitted with bells for premature burial victims is compelling, but it has no documented connection to the idiom.

Fun Fact: Victorian coffins did sometimes include safety features like breathing tubes and escape hatches, because the fear of premature burial was genuine. The phrase didn't come from that. The fear did.

5. "GO TO THE MAT"

To "go to the mat" means to fight hard for something and refuse to back down. The phrase comes from wrestling, where the match ends when someone is pinned. It expanded into everyday language by the 20th century and became common in legal and political reporting in the 1970s to describe any high-stakes, no-retreat confrontation.

Fun Fact: Wrestling is among the oldest documented sports in human history. Egyptian and Greek depictions of wrestlers go back over 4,000 years, which means people have been going to the mat for a very long time.

6. "THE BALL IS IN YOUR COURT"

The phrase means it's someone else's turn to act. It comes from tennis, where once a player hits the ball over the net, the responsibility to return it shifts entirely to the opponent. The phrase moved into business, politics, and personal situations by the early 20th century as shorthand for transferred responsibility.

Fun Fact: Tennis has produced one of the longest matches in sports history: the 2010 Wimbledon match between John Isner and Nicolas Mahut lasted 11 hours and 5 minutes across three days. The ball was in someone's court for a very long time.

7. "HAIL MARY PASS"

A "Hail Mary pass" is a desperate, last-minute attempt with long odds and not much choice. The phrase comes from American football, where a quarterback with seconds left throws a long, risky pass and hopes. Catholic players had been saying actual Hail Mary prayers before big plays since the 1920s, but the phrase entered common use on December 28, 1975, when Roger Staubach described his game-winning throw: "I closed my eyes and said a Hail Mary." It has covered last-ditch efforts in business, relationships, and politics ever since.

Fun Fact: The longest successful Hail Mary in NFL history was 61 yards, thrown by Aaron Rodgers in 2015. He did not close his eyes.

8. "RUN INTERFERENCE"

To "run interference" means to clear obstacles for someone else so they can move forward. It comes from American football, where offensive players block defenders to open a path for the ball carrier. The phrase crossed into business and politics in the 20th century, covering anyone who steps in to deflect problems on someone else's behalf.

Fun Fact: The forward pass wasn't legal in football until 1906. Before that, running interference wasn't a strategy. It was the only option.

9. "JUMP THE GUN"

To "jump the gun" means to act before the right moment. The phrase comes from track and field, where a runner who starts before the starting pistol fires is disqualified for a false start. By the 1940s it had expanded to describe anyone rushing into something prematurely.

Fun Fact: The fastest recorded false start was 0.086 seconds after the gun fired, which is faster than the human nervous system can process a sound and react. The runner had to be anticipating the gun, not responding to it.

10. "NECK AND NECK"

"Neck and neck" describes two competitors so evenly matched that neither has a clear lead. The phrase comes from horse racing, where two horses running side by side appear to have their necks perfectly aligned. It has been in racing terminology since at least the early 19th century and has since covered tight political races, close business competition, and any finish too close to call.

Fun Fact: The 2018 Pegasus World Cup came down to photo-finish technology to separate the top two horses by millimeters. Neck and neck is not always a metaphor.

11. "TEE IT UP"

To "tee it up" means to prepare something for action. The phrase comes from golf, where a player sets the ball on a tee before the first swing. It moved into figurative use in the early 20th century, covering the setup of ideas, proposals, and topics before launching into them.

Fun Fact: Before the tee existed, golfers built small mounds of sand to rest the ball on. The tee didn't become standard until the late 1800s. Preparation has always required some assembly.

12. "FULL-COURT PRESS"

A "full-court press" means an aggressive, all-out effort that gives the opponent no room to breathe. It comes from basketball, where a defensive strategy applies pressure across the entire court rather than just near the basket. The phrase spread into business, politics, and media in the mid-20th century to describe any relentless push toward a goal.

Fun Fact: John Wooden's UCLA Bruins used the full-court press to anchor a run of 10 NCAA championships in 12 years in the 1960s. The strategy was suffocating enough to work at the highest level.

13. "GAME OF INCHES"

The phrase means that tiny differences determine outcomes, in sports and everywhere else. It comes from American football, where a game can turn on a first down measurement, a missed field goal, or a play that falls short by less than a foot. It moved into broader use through sports broadcasting and became a metaphor for any situation where small details carry disproportionate weight.

Fun Fact: Al Pacino's halftime speech in *Any Given Sunday* (1999) built an entire monologue around the phrase. The longest field goal in NFL history was 64 yards. One inch in either direction can end a season.

14. "COVER ALL THE BASES"

To "cover all the bases" means to be fully prepared for every possible outcome. The phrase comes from baseball, where fielders guard each base to prevent the opposing team from advancing. It became a standard business and political phrase in the mid-20th century for any situation requiring thorough preparation.

Fun Fact: Baseball bases are exactly 90 feet apart, a distance that has remained unchanged because it produces the closest balance between offense and defense. The margin for error built into the field is part of the design.

15. "IN THE BIG LEAGUES"

To be "in the big leagues" means to operate at the highest level of competition. The phrase comes from Major League Baseball, which represents the top tier of professional play. It moved into figurative use in the early 1900s to describe anyone who had climbed from minor status into major, high-stakes territory.

Fun Fact: A player officially enters the big leagues when added to a team's 40-man roster, making them eligible for call-up to the majors. The threshold is specific, which is part of why the phrase carries weight.

16. "PLAY HARDBALL"

To "play hardball" means to act aggressively and without compromise to get what you want. The phrase comes from baseball, where a regulation hardball is faster and more dangerous than the softer alternative used in slow-pitch. By the 1970s it had moved into business and politics as shorthand for tough negotiations and refusal to back down.

Fun Fact: A major league fastball can top 100 mph. The metaphor of hardball as dangerous and unforgiving is not much of a stretch.

17. "BATTING A THOUSAND"

To be "batting a thousand" means to have a perfect streak of success. The phrase comes from baseball batting averages, where 1.000 would mean hitting successfully every single time at bat. The phrase moved into everyday use in the 20th century to describe anyone on an unbroken winning run.

Fun Fact: No MLB player has ever finished a full season batting 1.000. John Paciorek came closest by going 3-for-3 in his only Major League appearance in 1963. He never played another game. The record stands unchallenged for reasons that are mostly sad.

18. "DOWN TO THE WIRE"

"Down to the wire" means a competition stays uncertain until the very last moment. The phrase comes from horse racing, where a thin wire stretched across the finish line determined the winner. It was first recorded in 1889 and expanded into sports, politics, and business to cover any contest where the outcome isn't settled until the end.

Fun Fact: Before photo-finish technology, human judges called horse race results by eye. Races that truly came down to the wire produced arguments that the wire itself couldn't settle.

19. "THROW A CURVEBALL"

To "throw a curveball" means to surprise someone with something they didn't see coming. The phrase comes from baseball, where a curveball shifts direction mid-flight, making it difficult to track and nearly impossible to predict. It appeared figuratively in the mid-20th century for any unexpected challenge or twist.

Fun Fact: A well-thrown curveball can break up to 17 inches from where it appeared to be heading. Batters know it's coming and still can't always adjust in time.

20. "Hanging by a Thread"

To be "hanging by a thread" means to be one step from disaster. The phrase traces to the legend of the Sword of Damocles, where a ruler let Damocles experience luxury and power, but with a sword suspended above him by a single hair, making the threat of ruin impossible to ignore. The phrase became standard in sports, business, and politics for anyone barely holding their position.

Fun Fact: Competitive rock climbers sometimes hold their entire body weight on a single fingerhold. The thread in the legend was a metaphor. In climbing, it is closer to a literal description.

CHAPTER SIX

WE THE PEOPLE

1. "THE BUCK STOPS HERE"

"The buck stops here" means taking full responsibility rather than passing it to someone else. The phrase was popularized by Harry S. Truman, who kept a sign with those words on his desk as a reminder that the decisions of his administration were his alone. It connects to the poker term "passing the buck," where a marker was moved to indicate whose turn it was to deal, and whose responsibility it was to handle the game.

Fun Fact: Truman's sign was a gift from a prison warden. It now sits in the Harry S. Truman Presidential Library, which is either fitting or ironic depending on your politics.

2. "CROSS THE RUBICON"

To "cross the Rubicon" means to pass the point of no return. The phrase comes from 49 BC, when Julius Caesar led his army across the Rubicon River in defiance of the Roman Senate, an act that constituted a declaration of war. Once he crossed, there was no reversing the decision. It led directly to civil war, the fall of the Roman Republic, and the rise of the Empire.

Fun Fact: The Rubicon River still exists in northern Italy. It is considerably smaller than the weight of its history would suggest.

3. "LET THEM EAT CAKE"

The phrase describes someone completely out of touch with ordinary people's struggles. It is attributed to Marie Antoinette, but there is no evidence she said it. The phrase first appeared in Rousseau's *Confessions* (1765), where an unnamed "great princess" suggests the poor eat brioche when they have no bread. The association with Marie Antoinette came later, most likely as revolutionary propaganda designed to make her seem contemptuous of the poor.

Fun Fact: The original French phrase is "Qu'ils mangent de la brioche." Brioche is not cake. It is an enriched, buttery bread that was more expensive than ordinary loaves, which is the point, but the mistranslation outlasted the correction by centuries.

4. "READ THE RIOT ACT"

To "read the riot act" means to deliver a stern warning with real consequences attached. The phrase comes from an actual British law, the Riot Act of 1714, which required an official to read a specific passage aloud to any unlawful gathering. If the crowd didn't disperse within an hour, they could be arrested or killed. The phrase moved into everyday use as a metaphor for any serious warning delivered by someone with authority.

Fun Fact: The Riot Act remained on the books until 1973. For over 250 years, it was technically a legal option in the UK.

5. "BURY THE HATCHET"

To "bury the hatchet" means to make peace and leave a conflict behind. The phrase comes from Native American customs, particularly among the Iroquois and other Eastern Woodland tribes, where chiefs literally buried a war hatchet as a formal act of peace between warring groups. European writers documented the practice in the 1600s, and the phrase entered American political and diplomatic language in the 18th and 19th centuries.

Fun Fact: In 1784, following the American Revolution, Native American leaders and U.S. officials performed an actual hatchet-burying ceremony during treaty negotiations. The metaphor was still the literal thing.

6. "BEHIND THE EIGHT BALL"

To be "behind the eight ball" means to be stuck in a difficult position with few good options. The phrase comes from pool, where the eight ball must be sunk last. If your cue ball ends up behind the eight ball, your next shot becomes nearly impossible to execute cleanly. The phrase came out of American pool halls in the 1920s and 1930s and spread into business and politics as shorthand for being trapped.

Fun Fact: In some pool variations, sinking the eight ball at the wrong moment automatically loses the game. The eight ball is not neutral. It is either your salvation or your undoing.

7. "FIFTH COLUMN"

A "fifth column" refers to secret sympathizers working from within to undermine their own side. The phrase was coined during the Spanish Civil War by General Emilio Mola, who claimed he had four columns of soldiers attacking Madrid and a fifth column of supporters already inside the city. It spread quickly into wartime language and became standard in World War II and Cold War discussions of internal threats and saboteurs.

Fun Fact: The phrase still gets used today for corporate insiders, hackers, and political operatives working to destabilize organizations from within. The war is different. The column is the same.

8. "SPIN DOCTOR"

A "spin doctor" is a communications strategist who shapes how information is presented to make something look better than it is. The term emerged in American politics in the 1980s, when media handlers became skilled at reframing negative events for public consumption. The word "spin" comes from the idea of putting a deliberate rotation on something to change where it lands.

Fun Fact: One of the earliest recognized spin moments came during the 1984 presidential debate, when Ronald Reagan's team turned concerns about his age into a punchline that landed well enough to defuse the issue entirely.

9. "A House Divided"

The phrase describes an organization or group so internally fractured that it cannot hold together. It comes from the Bible, Mark 3:25, where Jesus states that a house divided against itself cannot stand. Abraham Lincoln used it in an 1858 speech about slavery, warning that the United States could not survive permanently half-slave and half-free. The phrase has anchored political and organizational warnings ever since.

Fun Fact: Lincoln's "House Divided" speech alarmed some of his own allies, who considered it too inflammatory. He gave it anyway.

10. "Bread and Circuses"

"Bread and circuses" describes the practice of keeping a population compliant through entertainment and basic provision rather than meaningful governance. The phrase comes from the Roman poet Juvenal, writing around 100 AD, who criticized politicians for pacifying citizens with free grain and public spectacles instead of addressing the empire's real problems. The critique has never really gone out of date.

Fun Fact: The Roman Colosseum was a centerpiece of the bread and circuses strategy, offering gladiator combat, animal fights, and chariot races while the empire deteriorated around it. The crowds kept coming anyway.

11. "Throw in the Towel"

To "throw in the towel" means to give up or admit defeat. The phrase comes from boxing, where a trainer would literally throw a towel into the ring to signal their fighter couldn't continue. The practice began in the late 19th century, when cornermen were permitted to surrender on a fighter's behalf.

Fun Fact: The original phrase was "throw up the sponge." Boxers used water-soaked sponges to clean wounds between rounds before towels became standard. The sponge lost the branding battle.

12. "Iron Curtain"

The "Iron Curtain" described the political and ideological divide between Communist Eastern Europe and the democratic West during the Cold War. Winston Churchill put the phrase into wide circulation in a 1946 speech warning that Soviet influence had dropped a barrier across the continent. The phrase became the defining image of Cold War division. The Iron Curtain fell in 1989 when Communist governments collapsed across Eastern Europe.

Fun Fact: The Berlin Wall was the most visible physical manifestation of the Iron Curtain, but Churchill's phrase originally referred to ideology and censorship, not concrete and wire. The wall came later and made it literal.

13. "Wag the Dog"

"Wag the dog" means using a minor or manufactured distraction to draw attention away from a larger problem. The image is a tail controlling the dog rather than the other way around. The phrase entered mainstream use after the 1997 film *Wag the Dog*, which depicted a fabricated war staged to cover a presidential scandal, but the concept had been in political and media use since at least the 19th century.

Fun Fact: The phrase gets applied regularly to political campaigns and crisis management whenever a government or company is suspected of staging a distraction. The accusation is easier to make than to prove. That's part of why it keeps working.

14. "NAPOLEON COMPLEX"

A "Napoleon complex" describes someone who compensates for small stature with aggressive or domineering behavior. It is named after Napoleon Bonaparte, though Napoleon was not particularly short. He stood around 5'6" by modern measurement, average for his era. The misconception came from British propaganda that exaggerated his height to mock his ambition and make him seem ridiculous.

Fun Fact: Studies have found no consistent evidence that shorter men are more aggressive. The stereotype came from propaganda, got repeated, and became its own kind of fact.

15. "GERRYMANDERING"

To "gerrymander" means to draw voting district boundaries in a way that gives one party an unfair advantage. The term comes from Elbridge Gerry, who in 1812 approved a Massachusetts redistricting map that heavily favored his party. One district was so oddly shaped that critics said it resembled a salamander. Gerry plus salamander became gerrymander, and the term has described manipulated electoral maps ever since.

Fun Fact: The original 1812 cartoon depicting the district showed a winged, snake-like creature to illustrate how unnatural the boundaries were. The drawing made the argument faster than the text did.

16. "Rob Peter to Pay Paul"

To "rob Peter to pay Paul" means to solve one problem by creating another, particularly in financial matters. The phrase dates to the 14th century, when money was reportedly transferred from St. Peter's Church in Westminster to cover debts owed to St. Paul's Cathedral in London. By the 16th century it had become a general metaphor for shifting resources without actually resolving anything.

Fun Fact: Shakespeare used a version of the phrase in *Henry IV, Part 2* (1597), which helped cement it in common English use. The problem it describes has never gone away.

17. "Trial by Fire"

To go through a "trial by fire" means to be tested under extreme pressure with no easy exit. The phrase comes from medieval judicial ordeals, where accused individuals walked across hot coals or held red-hot iron. Survival or miraculous healing was taken as proof of innocence, on the theory that divine intervention would protect the just. By the 17th century the phrase had become a metaphor for any situation that tests someone through sheer intensity.

Fun Fact: One of the earliest recorded trials by fire occurred in the Holy Roman Empire in 1068, when a woman accused of theft walked barefoot over red-hot plowshares. According to the records, she emerged unscathed. The records were kept by people with an interest in the system working.

18. "Don't Fire Until You See the Whites of Their Eyes"

The phrase means to hold back until the precise moment when action will have maximum effect. It comes from the Battle of Bunker Hill (1775), where Colonel William Prescott allegedly ordered his troops to wait until the British were close enough to make every shot count. The American militia had limited ammunition. Firing too early meant losing the fight before it started.

Fun Fact: Some historians believe the phrase was used in European warfare before the American Revolution and that Prescott may have been repeating a known tactical instruction rather than coining something new. The quote found its man regardless.

19. "Shot Heard 'Round the World"

The phrase describes a single event with consequences that ripple far beyond its origin. It comes from the first shots fired at the Battles of Lexington and Concord on April 19, 1775, the opening of the American Revolution. The phrase itself was coined by Ralph Waldo Emerson in his 1837 poem "Concord Hymn": "Here once the embattled farmers stood, / And fired the shot heard 'round the world."

Fun Fact: The phrase was borrowed by baseball in 1951 for Bobby Thomson's pennant-winning home run, which was broadcast live on radio to a national audience. Emerson's farmers would have found that puzzling.

20. "DAMN THE TORPEDOES!"

"Damn the torpedoes!" means charging ahead despite serious risks. The phrase comes from the Battle of Mobile Bay in 1864, when Admiral David Farragut was warned that Confederate underwater mines, then called torpedoes, could destroy his fleet. According to accounts, he responded: "Damn the torpedoes! Full speed ahead!" The charge succeeded and became one of the key Union naval victories of the Civil War.

Fun Fact: Some historians question whether Farragut said it exactly that way, or whether the wording was cleaned up afterward. Either way, he did order the fleet forward into the minefield. The quote may be approximate. The mines were real.

CHAPTER SEVEN

OUR WEATHER FOR TODAY

1. "Blow Hot and Cold"

To "blow hot and cold" means to be inconsistent, particularly in opinions or commitments. The phrase comes from Aesop's fable "The Man and the Satyr," where a man blows on his hands to warm them, then blows on his soup to cool it. The satyr, watching both, refuses to trust someone whose breath serves two opposite purposes. By the 16th century the phrase had settled into a metaphor for unpredictable behavior in relationships and politics.

Fun Fact: Latin had a version of the same idea: "fluctuare inter duo," meaning to waver between two extremes. The complaint about inconsistency is at least as old as Rome.

2. "EVERY CLOUD HAS A SILVER LINING"

The phrase means that even bad situations contain something worth holding onto. It traces to John Milton's *Comus* (1634), where he described a dark storm cloud turning out its silver lining against the night sky. The image became a visual metaphor for hope, and the phrase has been in common use as an expression of optimism ever since.

Fun Fact: British soldiers used the phrase during World War II to sustain morale. Milton wrote it for a masque performed at a castle. The phrase traveled further than he planned.

3. "FAIR-WEATHER FRIEND"

A fair-weather friend shows up when things are easy and disappears when they aren't. The phrase comes from sailing culture, where fair weather meant smooth passage and storms meant real danger. By the 19th century "fair-weather" had become a general modifier for anything unreliable under pressure. The phrase appeared in print in 1871 to describe politicians who shifted loyalties based on convenience.

Fun Fact: Some cultures use "sunshine friend" for the same idea. Someone who's present for the good weather and gone before the first cloud appears.

4. "RAIN ON SOMEONE'S PARADE"

To "rain on someone's parade" means to spoil their good mood or plans. The phrase comes from actual parades, where bad weather reliably destroys the atmosphere. The idiom existed before the 1960s but entered mainstream culture through "Don't Rain on My Parade" from the 1964 Broadway musical *Funny Girl*. Barbra

Streisand's performance made it unavoidable, and the phrase has been standard ever since.

Fun Fact: German uses "throwing water on the fire" for the same idea. French goes with cutting someone's grass from under their feet. Rain on a parade is apparently a universal concept with local weather.

5. "Throw Caution to the Wind"

To "throw caution to the wind" means to abandon careful planning and take a bold risk. The phrase comes from sailing, where ignoring wind conditions was considered genuinely reckless. It appeared in English literature in the late 19th century and was in wide use by the early 20th.

Fun Fact: Chinese has a similar image: releasing a kite with no string, letting go of control entirely. The wind is a consistent metaphor for things beyond your management.

6. "Chasing Rainbows"

To "chase rainbows" means to pursue something that can never actually be reached. The phrase comes from the ancient belief that a pot of gold lies at the end of a rainbow. Since rainbows are optical illusions, their end moves as you approach it, making the pursuit literally impossible. The phrase became common in 19th-century poetry and literature and settled into everyday use as a metaphor for any futile goal.

Fun Fact: The pot of gold comes from Leprechaun mythology, where mischievous fairies hide treasure at a location no human can ever reach. The folklore and the physics agree on the outcome.

7. "Steal Someone's Thunder"

To "steal someone's thunder" means to take attention or credit away from someone else. The phrase has a specific theatrical origin: in the early 1700s, playwright John Dennis invented a stage effect to simulate thunder for his play. The play failed. Later, he discovered that other productions had borrowed his sound effect without permission. He reportedly said: "They will not let my play run, but they steal my thunder." The phrase caught on and by the 19th century had become a metaphor for upstaging anyone.

Fun Fact: Before Dennis' invention, thunder effects were created by shaking large metal sheets backstage. Less precise, but probably just as loud.

8. "Break the Ice"

To "break the ice" means to ease tension or get a conversation started. The phrase dates to the 16th century, when ships sailing through frozen waters literally had to break through ice to clear a path forward. Sir Thomas North used it metaphorically in 1579: "To break the ice and to make way for others." By the 19th century it had fully converted to social use.

Fun Fact: The word "icebreaker," as in icebreaker games or questions, comes directly from this idiom. The ships came first.

9. "Come Rain or Shine"

"Come rain or shine" means doing something regardless of obstacles or conditions. The phrase comes from farming and outdoor labor, where work continued whether the weather cooperated or not. It gained traction as an expression of determination in the

19th century and later became common in event advertising for anything that would proceed no matter what.

Fun Fact: Spanish has "against wind and tide" for the same idea. The specific weather varies. The stubbornness is constant.

10. "Lightning Never Strikes Twice"

The phrase suggests that the same unlikely event won't repeat itself. Science disagrees. Lightning regularly strikes the same location multiple times, particularly tall structures. The phrase came from 19th-century assumptions about lightning being random and unpredictable. It became a metaphor for reassuring people after bad luck or cautioning them against expecting repeated good fortune.

Fun Fact: The Empire State Building is struck by lightning roughly 25 times a year. The phrase is wrong about the physics and has been for a long time. It persists anyway.

11. "On Cloud Nine"

To be "on cloud nine" means to feel euphoric. The most widely cited origin traces to meteorological cloud classification, where cumulonimbus clouds were designated Cloud No. 9 in the International Cloud Atlas, the highest and most dramatic clouds in the sky. Since height has long been associated with happiness and elation, the ninth cloud became a shorthand for floating in joy.

Fun Fact: An earlier version, "cloud seven," circulated in the 1930s. Cloud nine overtook it for reasons nobody has fully explained. Seven was already taken by luck, which may have helped.

12. "MAKE HAY WHILE THE SUN SHINES"

The phrase means to take advantage of good conditions before they change. It comes from actual haymaking, which required dry, sunny weather. Before modern machinery, farmers who missed the window and let rain in could lose the harvest entirely. Speed during good weather wasn't a preference. It was the difference between having feed and not having it. The phrase entered English in the 16th century and became standard advice for seizing any opportunity before circumstances shift.

Fun Fact: "Strike while the iron is hot" covers the same ground from a blacksmithing angle. Different trades, same lesson.

13. "SNOWED UNDER"

To be "snowed under" means to be buried under more work or responsibility than you can manage. The phrase comes from actual snowfall, where heavy accumulation could immobilize entire communities and make keeping up with ordinary life impossible. By the 19th century it had moved into business and academic use as a metaphor for anyone overwhelmed by deadlines or obligations.

Fun Fact: Buffalo, New York in 1977 saw snowdrifts reach 30 feet. The city was functionally buried. The metaphor has a credible basis in fact.

14. "THE WINDS OF CHANGE"

To feel "the winds of change" means to sense that something significant is shifting. Wind was one of the earliest signals of approaching weather in sailing and agriculture, making it a natural metaphor for coming transformation. The phrase entered modern political language most prominently through Harold Macmillan's 1960 speech on African decolonization: "The wind of change is blowing through this continent."

Fun Fact: The Scorpions built a 1990 hit around the same phrase, writing "Wind of Change" about the fall of the Berlin Wall. Macmillan's speech and a German rock band ended up describing the same half-century of history.

15. "Storm in a Teacup"

To call something "a storm in a teacup" means making a dramatic fuss over something minor. The phrase traces to Cicero, who used a similar image: "Excitabat fluctus in simpulo," meaning he stirred up waves in a ladle. The expression developed into its current form in 18th-century Britain, where the teacup provided an appropriately small container to contrast with a storm.

Fun Fact: Americans say "tempest in a teapot." French goes with "storm in a glass of water." The vessel shrinks, the overreaction stays the same.

16. "Take the Wind Out of Someone's Sails"

To "take the wind out of someone's sails" means to deflate their confidence or momentum. The phrase comes from naval warfare, where a ship could position itself to block the wind reaching an enemy vessel, causing it to lose speed and control. The tactic was standard in the Age of Sail and by the 19th century had become a metaphor for anything that knocks the energy out of someone.

Fun Fact: Horatio Nelson's most famous victories depended partly on wind tactics, maneuvering to control airflow before the fighting started. The metaphor was once a battle plan.

17. "WEATHER THE STORM"

To "weather the storm" means to endure a difficult situation and come out the other side. The phrase comes from seafaring, where surviving a violent storm required skill, patience, and a degree of luck. By the 18th century it had become a general metaphor for pushing through personal, financial, or political hardship.

Fun Fact: Some ancient sailors believed that sacrificing livestock to sea gods would calm the waters. Weathering the storm had a transactional dimension before it became a metaphor.

18. "BOLT FROM THE BLUE"

A "bolt from the blue" describes something sudden and completely unexpected. The phrase comes from the rare phenomenon of lightning appearing from a clear sky, with no visible storm to explain it. The phrase gained traction in the 19th century as a description for any shock that arrives without warning.

Fun Fact: Blue sky lightning is real. A bolt can travel more than 10 miles from its originating storm and strike in apparently clear conditions. The idiom is not much of an exaggeration.

19. "CAUGHT IN THE EYE OF THE STORM"

To be in 'the eye of the storm' means to be at the center of chaos or controversy. The phrase comes from hurricanes, where the eye is a deceptively calm area surrounded by the storm's most violent winds. Sailors who entered the eye experienced a brief and misleading peace before the storm returned. By the 19th century the phrase described anyone in the middle of a crisis.

Fun Fact: The largest recorded hurricane eye was 125 miles wide. An entire metropolitan area could sit inside it before the storm closed back in.

20. "QUICK AS LIGHTNING"

"Quick as lightning" means extraordinarily fast. The phrase draws on the actual speed of lightning, which travels at roughly 220,000 miles per hour, fast enough that there is no practical human reaction time. It appeared in poetry and literature by at least the 18th century as a description for swift actions, decisions, or reflexes.

Fun Fact: The longest lightning bolt ever recorded traveled approximately 477 miles, from Texas to Mississippi. Fast and far.

CHAPTER EIGHT

KA-CHING!

1. "Nest Egg"

A "nest egg" refers to money saved for the future. The phrase dates to the 17th century, when farmers placed a fake egg in a hen's nest to encourage her to lay more. The association between planting something now to produce more later carried over into financial language, and by the 19th century "nest egg" meant savings. By the 20th century it was standard in banking and retirement planning.

Fun Fact: The fake egg trick and long-term investing operate on the same basic logic. Leave something in place, wait, and hope it multiplies.

2. "KEEPING UP WITH THE JONESES"

The phrase describes the pressure to match neighbors in wealth and possessions. It comes from a 1913 comic strip by Arthur R. "Pop" Momand, which satirized a family's constant struggle to compete with their unseen, supposedly affluent neighbors. The Joneses were never shown. The anxiety they produced was the whole point.

Some point to Jones Street in Savannah, Georgia, one of the wealthiest and most admired addresses in the city's historic district, as a possible real-world inspiration. Tour guides have claimed the connection for years, though the comic strip origin is better documented.

Fun Fact: Social media has produced a modern version where the Joneses are curated, filtered, and not entirely real. The pressure is the same. The neighbors are worse.

3. "A PENNY FOR YOUR THOUGHTS"

The phrase is an invitation to share what someone is thinking. It appeared in John Heywood's proverb collection in 1546, and at the time a penny carried enough value to make the offer feel genuine. The idiom has stayed in use for nearly 500 years, though the economic logic has not aged as well.

Fun Fact: In Shakespeare's day, a penny bought a standing ticket to the theater. Offering one for someone's thoughts was a reasonable trade at the time. Today it costs considerably more to get into a show, and nobody is offering pennies for anything.

4. "Go for Broke"

To "go for broke" means to risk everything on one attempt. The phrase comes from gambling, where betting everything on a single hand means either winning big or losing it all. It gained its most significant association during World War II, when the 442nd Infantry Regiment, a Japanese American unit, adopted it as their motto. The 442nd became one of the most decorated units in U.S. military history.

Fun Fact: The 1951 film *Go for Broke!* told the regiment's story and helped cement both the phrase and the unit's legacy in American culture.

5. "A Fool and His Money Are Soon Parted"

The proverb means that careless people lose their wealth quickly. It first appeared in print in John Bridges' *Defence of the Government of the Church of England* (1587): "A fool and his money be soon at debate, which after with sorrow repents him too late." The warning has been applied to scams, bad investments, and impulsive spending ever since.

Fun Fact: Benjamin Franklin included variations of the phrase in *Poor Richard's Almanack*, which helped spread it widely in America. Franklin had opinions about money and was not shy about sharing them.

6. "Throw Money Down the Drain"

To "throw money down the drain" means to waste money on something useless. The phrase comes from the literal image of dropping coins into a drain, where they are gone for good. It appeared in the 19th century as indoor plumbing became common, and warnings about valuables slipping into drains were practical before they became metaphorical.

Fun Fact: Archaeologists have found ancient coins in Roman drains. Some people were literally throwing money away long before the phrase existed.

7. "CASH COW"

A "cash cow" is a product, business, or investment that generates steady profit with minimal ongoing effort. The phrase comes from dairy farming, where a well-kept cow produces milk reliably over time. The term moved into financial language in the 1960s when analysts applied it to products that required little investment but delivered consistent returns.

Fun Fact: The phrase was popularized in business strategy models, including the Boston Consulting Group's "Growth-Share Matrix," which classified companies' assets as Stars, Question Marks, Dogs, and Cash Cows.

8. "BURN THE CANDLE AT BOTH ENDS"

To "burn the candle at both ends" means to overwork yourself by pushing from both directions, too late at night and too early in the morning. The phrase comes from 17th-century France, where candles represented time and energy. Lighting both ends at once consumed them twice as fast. The phrase was translated into English in 1730 and became a standard description for anyone running themselves into the ground.

Fun Fact: Some historians trace the original meaning to reckless spending rather than overwork, since candles were expensive commodities and burning them wastefully was its own kind of foolishness.

9. "A Golden Handshake"

A "golden handshake" is a substantial financial package given to an employee, usually a senior executive, when they leave a company. It typically includes cash, stock options, or other benefits and is designed to ease the departure. The term was coined in Britain in the mid-1960s by Frederick Ellis, city editor of the *Daily Express*. It has generated controversy ever since, particularly when large payouts go to executives leaving companies that are performing poorly.

Fun Fact: The largest recorded golden handshake was approximately $53.8 million, awarded to F. Ross Johnson of RJR Nabisco in 1989. The payout became one of the central details of *Barbarians at the Gate*, the book about the takeover battle that followed.

10. "Jump on the Bandwagon"

To "jump on the bandwagon" means to follow a trend primarily because everyone else is. The phrase comes from 19th-century traveling circuses and political campaigns, where a wagon carrying a live band led the parade and drew a crowd. In 1848, politician Dan Rice used a bandwagon to promote his presidential campaign and invited supporters to jump on. The phrase expanded from there to cover any situation where people adopt an idea out of momentum rather than conviction.

Fun Fact: The phrase gets applied to marketing, politics, and social media with equal regularity. The bandwagon is always rolling. The music is just different.

11. "A DIME A DOZEN"

To say something is "a dime a dozen" means it is common and not particularly valuable. The phrase comes from 19th-century American marketplaces, where vendors sold bulk goods at a dime for twelve. Since these items were cheap and widely available, the phrase became a metaphor for anything ordinary or easily replaced. It appeared in American newspapers by the 1860s and was in wide use by the 20th century.

Fun Fact: Historical ads listed dozens of items at a dime, including postcards, fishhooks, and sewing needles. The pricing was real before it became a metaphor.

12. "FEAST OR FAMINE"

"Feast or famine" describes situations of extreme highs and lows, particularly in money or work. The phrase comes from agricultural societies where harvests determined everything: a good year meant abundance, a bad year meant shortage. It appeared in English literature in the 17th century and gained renewed relevance during the Great Depression, when entire industries swung between booms and collapse.

Fun Fact: The entertainment industry uses the phrase so often it has become a cliche within the cliche. Actors and musicians live the feast or famine cycle reliably enough that it stopped being a metaphor.

13. "GREASE SOMEONE'S PALM"

To "grease someone's palm" means to bribe them. The phrase dates to at least the 16th century, when "grease" was slang for wealth and smooth dealings. A greased palm was a paid one. Shakespeare used it in *King John* (1597): "I will grease his palms with good store of gold."

Fun Fact: Some historians trace the phrase to ancient Rome, where politicians and merchants reportedly oiled their hands before financial transactions. The metaphor may have started as a literal practice.

14. "A Penny Saved Is a Penny Earned"

The phrase means that saving money is as valuable as making it. It is commonly credited to Benjamin Franklin, but he never said it in quite those words. In his 1737 *Poor Richard's Almanack*, he wrote "A penny saved is two pence clear." The simplified version that stuck came later, but the underlying argument was his: avoiding unnecessary spending is functionally the same as increasing income.

Fun Fact: Each penny cost more to produce than its face value for years before production finally stopped. Franklin's thrift proverb became an argument for ending the coin entirely.

15. "Put Your Money Where Your Mouth Is"

To "put your money where your mouth is" means to back up words with action, usually a financial commitment. The phrase originated in early 20th-century America, in gambling, politics, and sports, where it challenged people to prove confidence by placing real money on their claims. It expanded from betting into a general push for people to support beliefs and causes with action rather than talk.

Fun Fact: Charities and social movements use it constantly as a pointed way of asking whether someone's stated values and their actual spending match. Usually, they don't.

16. "BALLPARK FIGURE"

A "ballpark figure" means a rough estimate rather than a precise number. The phrase comes from American baseball, where a ball lands somewhere within the ballpark but not in any specific spot. The metaphor for approximation caught on in the 1940s and 1950s, particularly in business and finance where quick estimates mattered more than exact figures.

Fun Fact: The phrase is standard in real estate, car sales, and government budgets, where an opening estimate sets expectations before the actual numbers arrive and disappoint everyone.

17. "WOLF OF WALL STREET"

The term describes a ruthless, aggressive investor willing to use unethical means to profit. The phrase was in use in the 1980s and 1990s to describe predatory stock traders and corporate raiders before the 2013 film brought it to a wider audience. Jordan Belfort, whose fraud schemes inspired the movie, adopted the label himself.

Fun Fact: The phrase also gets applied to high-risk investors who operate aggressively but legally, which suggests the wolf has become more of a personality type than a criminal designation.

18. "A Rising Tide Lifts All Boats"

The phrase means that broad improvement benefits everyone, not just those at the top. It comes from New England fishing communities, where a rising tide literally floated all vessels higher. John F. Kennedy adopted it in the 1960s to argue that economic growth would benefit all social classes, and the association stuck.

Fun Fact: Kennedy didn't coin it. The phrase was already circulating through chamber of commerce speeches before he picked it up. He just had a better platform.

19. "The Sky's the Limit"

"The sky's the limit" means there is no ceiling on what can be achieved. The phrase emerged in early 20th-century aviation, when altitude records were being broken regularly and the idea of human flight was still new enough to feel like proof that anything was possible. It became a standard expression of ambition in the 1920s and 1930s.

Fun Fact: Astronauts have pointed out that the sky is no longer the limit in any literal sense, which either updates the phrase or ruins it depending on your perspective.

20. "Midas Touch"

The "Midas touch" means the ability to generate wealth or success seemingly without effort. It comes from the Greek myth of King Midas, who asked the god Dionysus to turn everything he touched to gold. It worked on twigs and stones. It also worked on his food, his drink, and in some versions of the myth, his daughter. Midas asked Dionysus to take the gift back. He was told to bathe in the river Pactolus, which removed the curse and, according to legend, left the river's sands rich with gold.

Fun Fact: King Midas appears in multiple myths. In another, he judged a music contest between Apollo and Pan, picked the wrong winner, and was given donkey ears as punishment. The golden touch was not his only bad decision.

CHAPTER NINE

FASHIONABLY LATE TO THE IDIOM PARTY

1. "As Fit as a Fiddle"

To be "as fit as a fiddle" means to be in excellent health. The phrase dates to the early 17th century, when "fit" meant suitable or appropriate rather than physically strong. The original meaning was closer to "perfectly suited," like a well-tuned violin ready to play. Over time it shifted to describe a person's physical condition specifically.

Fun Fact: The fiddle has long been associated with quickness and agility in folk music traditions, which may have helped nudge the phrase toward physical fitness over time. Or it may just be the alliteration. Nobody is entirely sure.

2. "Back to Square One"

To "go back to square one" means to start over completely. For a phrase this common, the origin is genuinely uncertain, which is either humbling or amusing depending on your disposition.

The board game theory points to Snakes and Ladders, where a bad roll sends a player to the beginning. The problem: most versions don't actually return players to the first square. The BBC football theory suggests that 1920s radio commentators divided the pitch into numbered squares to help listeners follow the action. The problem: no recorded evidence exists that anyone actually used the phrase on air. The hopscotch theory has the least support of all three.

Fun Fact: The phrase is used constantly in science, business, and technology to describe failed experiments and abandoned plans. The origin of the phrase itself remains unsolved. It is, in a sense, still at square one.

3. "The Whole Nine Yards"

To go "the whole nine yards" means to give everything, hold nothing back. The origin is genuinely disputed. The most popular theory links it to World War II fighter pilots, whose machine gun ammunition belts measured 27 feet, or nine yards. Firing everything meant going the whole nine yards. Other theories involve Scottish kilts, fabric measurements, football fields, and concrete trucks. None have been proven. The phrase appeared in print in the 1960s and has been debated ever since.

Fun Fact: No written record of the phrase exists before the 1950s, which makes every theory about its earlier origin difficult to verify. It remains one of the more stubborn unsolved questions in etymology.

4. "Skeleton in the Closet"

A "skeleton in the closet" is a hidden secret, usually embarrassing or damaging. The phrase appeared in the early 19th century, possibly drawn from murder mysteries and gothic literature where concealed skeletons were a staple plot device. One theory places the origin in English medical schools, which illegally obtained human skeletons for research and kept them locked away to avoid legal trouble. By the mid-1800s the phrase had settled into a general metaphor for buried secrets.

Fun Fact: Some cultures use "a snake under the floor" for the same idea. Hidden, dangerous, and best left undisturbed.

5. "Raining Cats and Dogs"

To say it's "raining cats and dogs" means it's raining hard. The origin is genuinely uncertain. One theory connects it to Norse mythology, where cats symbolized storms and dogs symbolized wind. Another points to 17th-century England, where poor drainage caused dead animals to wash into the streets during heavy rain, creating the impression they had come from above. Jonathan Swift used related imagery in his 1710 poem "A Description of a City Shower," describing streets littered with drowned animals after a storm.

Fun Fact: The phrase has been in use for over 300 years and the origin is still debated. For something said so casually, it has generated a surprising amount of academic argument.

6. "GRAVY TRAIN"

To be "riding the gravy train" means making easy money with little effort, usually by exploiting access others don't have. The phrase comes from early 20th-century American railroad slang, where "gravy" described an easy or comfortable run. By the 1940s it had moved into politics and business as a description for officials and executives profiting from perks, loopholes, or public funds.

Fun Fact: The phrase gained particular traction in post-WWII journalism, where reporters used it to describe politicians and contractors enriching themselves on public money. The train metaphor made the accusation vivid enough to stick.

7. "A WILD GOOSE CHASE"

A "wild goose chase" means a futile pursuit that leads nowhere. Shakespeare used the phrase in *Romeo and Juliet* (1595), where it originally described a type of horse race in which riders had to mimic the unpredictable movements of the lead horse, resembling geese in flight. The racing meaning faded. The futility remained.

Fun Fact: Wild geese fly in shifting, unpredictable patterns that make them nearly impossible to follow. The metaphor chose its animal well.

8. "GO COLD TURKEY"

To "go cold turkey" means to quit something abruptly and completely, without tapering off. The phrase dates to the early 20th century and was first used in the context of addiction withdrawal. One theory connects it to the physical symptoms of withdrawal: pale, cold, goosebump-covered skin resembling a plucked

turkey. Another suggests it simply means stopping without preparation, the way cold turkey requires no cooking.

Fun Fact: The phrase was first recorded in 1921 in a Vancouver
newspaper, describing a politician who stopped talking abruptly.
The addiction meaning came later and eventually took over
entirely.

9. "Happy as a Clam"

To be "happy as a clam" means to be thoroughly content. The original phrase was "happy as a clam at high tide," meaning a clam is
safest from fishermen when the water is high. The full version was
first recorded in early 19th-century New England, where clam-
ming was common. The tide reference dropped away over time,
leaving just the clam and the happiness.

Fun Fact: Clams don't express emotions, but a slightly open shell
does look like a smile. The idiom may have survived partly on the
strength of that image.

10. "A Monkey on Your Back"

To have "a monkey on your back" means to carry a persistent
burden, problem, or addiction that won't let go. The phrase
appeared in the 19th century as a general description of heavy
burdens before narrowing into addiction slang in the early 20th
century. By the 1950s it was common in rehabilitation communities as a way of describing the grip of substance dependence. Over
time it widened again to cover any lingering problem that's hard
to shake.

Fun Fact: Some cultures use "a demon on your back" for the same idea. The monkey version is more universal. The demon version is more accurate.

11. "BARKING UP THE WRONG TREE"

To "bark up the wrong tree" means to pursue a mistaken course of action. The phrase comes from American hunting, where dogs chased prey into trees and sometimes barked at the wrong one, convinced the animal was still there when it had already moved on. It was first recorded in the 1830s in frontier communities before becoming a general metaphor for misplaced effort or false accusations.

Fun Fact: Spanish has "throwing stones at the wrong person" for the same idea. The effort is real. The target is just off.

12. "DEAD RINGER"

A "dead ringer" is an exact duplicate or someone who looks nearly identical to another person. The phrase comes from 19th-century horse racing, where dishonest gamblers entered a fast horse disguised as a slower one to deceive bookmakers. A ringer was the fraudulent substitute. A dead ringer was a perfect, undetectable one. The term moved from horses to people and has covered uncanny resemblances ever since.

Fun Fact: The phrase has nothing to do with graveyard bells or premature burial, despite a persistent myth to the contrary. Horse racing fraud is considerably less dramatic, but it is the actual origin.

13. "Have a Frog in Your Throat"

To "have a frog in your throat" means to have difficulty speaking due to hoarseness. The phrase appeared in the late 19th century as a description of that specific scratchy, obstructed feeling. Some connect it to folk remedies that involved gargling or drinking to flush out whatever was causing the problem. By the 20th century it was standard description for temporary voice loss.

Fun Fact: Medieval medicine occasionally involved placing live frogs in a patient's mouth to treat throat ailments. The phrase outlasted the practice by several centuries, which is probably for the best.

14. "A Cock and Bull Story"

A "cock and bull story" is an implausible, exaggerated tale, usually made up. One theory traces it to two famous English coaching inns, The Cock and The Bull, where travelers exchanged increasingly wild stories over drinks. Another connects it to Aesop's Fables, which featured talking animals including roosters and bulls, making the stories feel fantastical. By the 18th century the phrase was standard shorthand for any far-fetched claim, particularly in politics and gossip.

Fun Fact: The phrase still gets used for false alibis, exaggerated news, and dramatic storytelling. Some things travel well.

15. "A Red Herring"

A "red herring" is a distraction or false clue that pulls attention away from the real issue. The phrase comes from 18th-century British hunting, where smoked herrings were dragged across trails to test and train dogs by throwing them off the scent. Journalist

William Cobbett used it figuratively in 1807 to describe how politicians diverted public attention from real issues. The phrase found a natural home in mystery fiction and has been standard in crime, politics, and media ever since.

Fun Fact: Agatha Christie used red herrings so reliably that readers began to distrust every obvious suspect on principle. The technique became part of the genre's DNA.

16. "A Dog's Breakfast"

To call something "a dog's breakfast" means it's a complete mess. The phrase is British, dating to the late 19th century. A November 1878 review in *The Referee* used it to describe a play that crammed too much into too little space: "the good things are flung together in a heap like a dog's breakfast."

Fun Fact: "A dog's dinner" covers the same territory with a small distinction: it can also describe someone dressed in an absurdly flashy way. Same dog, different problem.

17. "All Hat and No Cattle"

The phrase describes someone who presents themselves as substantial but has nothing to back it up. It comes from Texas cowboy culture, where a hat signified rancher status. Owning cattle was the actual measure. Wearing the hat without the herd meant performing a role you hadn't earned.

Fun Fact: Cowboy culture contributed more idioms than most people realize. "Riding shotgun" and "betting the farm" both come from the same tradition of ranch and frontier life.

18. "A FEATHER IN YOUR CAP"

To have "a feather in your cap" means to have earned a notable honor. The practice of adding feathers to headwear as a mark of achievement appears across cultures: Native American warriors received feathers for bravery, medieval European knights placed them in helmets after valorous deeds, and Scottish and Welsh hunters awarded the first feather from a game bird to whoever made the kill.

Fun Fact: "Yankee Doodle" references the tradition directly: "stuck a feather in his cap and called it macaroni." In 18th-century slang, "macaroni" meant a fashionable person. The joke was that a single feather was enough to consider yourself stylish.

19. "HEARD IT THROUGH THE GRAPEVINE"

To "hear something through the grapevine" means to receive information informally, through rumor or secondhand sources. The phrase comes from the American Civil War era, when telegraph lines were strung loosely and haphazardly, resembling grapevines. Messages transmitted over these lines were frequently distorted or misheard, producing the rumors that spread quickly through communities.

Fun Fact: Marvin Gaye's 1968 recording took the phrase worldwide. It had been in common use for a century before the song. The song is why most people know it.

20. "THE BEE'S KNEES"

To call something "the bee's knees" means it's excellent. The phrase emerged in 1920s America as part of a trend for fanciful animal-related expressions: the cat's pajamas, the cat's whiskers, the elephant's instep. None of them meant anything literally. All of them meant the best. In the 18th century, "bee's knee" had actually meant something small or insignificant. The Roaring Twenties reversed that entirely.

Fun Fact: Bees do have knees, and they use the joints in their legs to pack pollen into small built-in carrying structures. The phrase was invented as nonsense. It turned out to be accurate.

CONCLUSION

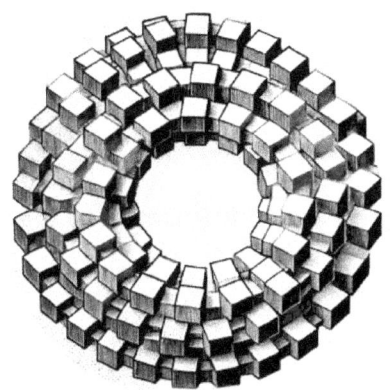

Here we are. Back to square one.

Except, of course, we don't actually know where square one came from.

Was it a board game? A football field? A misunderstanding that spiraled out of control? The answer is unclear.

If this book has done anything, it's shown that half the fun of language is figuring out where it all started.

One day, you might hear someone "jump on the bandwagon" and picture 19th-century politicians literally shouting from circus wagons, hoping people would hop aboard. And when someone says "the game is afoot," you'll know it started long before Sherlock ever pulled on his boots.

Language never sits still. The idioms we use today came from battlefields, theaters, sports, pop culture, and complete accidents. New ones are forming right now.

Keep listening. Keep questioning. Keep collecting.

Language is strange, specific, and occasionally ridiculous. And that's the whole point.

COMPLETE SERIES
BY EDDIE WATTS

SERIOUSLY THOUGH BOOKS

All three available on Amazon

ALSO AVAILABLE ON AUDIBLE

Yo, Sloth. I Got the Facts.
Random Trivia That'll Blow Your Mind
and Make You the Most Interesting Person
in the Room (Even if You're Shy)

Arrested for What Now:
A Global Guide to Bizarre Laws,
Curious Bans, and Moves You
Never Knew Were Illegal

THANK YOU FOR READING

ALSO AVAILABLE ON AUDIBLE

If you enjoyed Straight from the Llama's Mouth, a quick review on Amazon means more than you know.

Just a few words about what made you smile, laugh, or say, "Wait… what?"

It helps the next curious reader find their way here. You can search the title on Amazon, or simply scan the code below:

Thank you. Truly.

Eddie

SOURCES

18th-Century Business & Trade Archives. (n.d.). *Collected records from The British East India Company, The London Stock Exchange, and early merchant trading companies.*

18th-Century Farming & Travel Records. (n.d.). *Collected diaries and reports from British agricultural and trade societies.* National Archives UK.

18th-Century Farming & Veterinary Records. (n.d.). *Historical guides on animal husbandry, disease prevention, and agricultural medicine.* Royal Veterinary College, London.

19th-Century American Folklore Archives. (n.d.). *Compiled by The American Folklore Society, preserving regional tales, idioms, and cultural sayings.*

19th-Century American Newspaper Archives. (n.d.). Digitized by the Library of Congress. Available at chroniclingamerica.loc.gov

19th-Century American Slang Records. (n.d.). *Collection of regional slang and expressions.* Dictionary of American Regional English (DARE).

19th-Century British Parliamentary Records. (n.d.). Digitized by the UK National Archives, referencing debates and legislative decisions from the 1800s.

19th-Century British Shipbuilding Records. (n.d.). British Maritime & Dockyard Historical Society.

19th-Century British Social Customs Archives. (n.d.). *Documents on Victorian-era etiquette, traditions, and household practices.* British Library Social History Division.

19th-Century Russian Folklore Archives. (n.d.). *Compiled from Slavic oral traditions, fairy tales, and cultural proverbs.* Moscow State Library of Folklore Studies.

A dog's breakfast. (n.d.). In *The Phrase Finder*.

A dog's breakfast. (n.d.). In *Merriam-Webster.com Dictionary*.

A feather in one's cap. (n.d.). In The Phrase Finder. Retrieved from https://www.phrases.org.uk/meanings/a-feather-in-your-cap.html

A feather in your cap. (n.d.). In Wikipedia. Retrieved from https://en.wikipedia.org/wiki/A_feather_in_your_cap

As fit as a fiddle. (n.d.). In The Phrase Finder. Retrieved from https://www.phrases.org.uk/meanings/as-fit-as-a-fiddle.html

Aesop. (2002). *Aesop's fables* (L. Gibbs, Trans.). Oxford University Press. (Original work published 6th century BC)

Alger, H. (1868). *Ragged Dick.* Loring.

Ammer, C. (2013). *The American Heritage dictionary of idioms* (2nd ed.). Houghton Mifflin Harcourt.

Ancient Greek Election Records. (n.d.). *Documentation of voting practices and secret ballot methods.* Hellenic Parliament Archives.

Ancient Greek Fables & Mythology Archives. (n.d.). *Compiled texts from Hesiod, Aesop, and Greek Oral Traditions.* Hellenic Folklore Society.

Ancient Indian Religious Texts. (n.d.). *Collected scriptures from the Vedas, Upanishads, and Buddhist Pali Canon.* Indira Gandhi National Centre for the Arts.

Annenberg Classroom. (n.d.). Dark horse. Retrieved March 4, 2025, from https://www.annenbergclassroom.org/glossary_term/dark-horse/

Archaeological Reports on Ancient Rome. (n.d.). *Findings from The Italian Ministry of Culture and The British School at Rome.*

Aristotle. (2000). *Poetics* (T. S. Dorsch, Trans.). Penguin Classics. (Original work published ca. 335 BCE)

Arno, P. (1941, March 1). Well, back to the old drawing board [Cartoon]. *The New Yorker.* Retrieved March 4, 2025, from https://www.phrases.org.uk/meanings/back-to-the-drawing-board.html

Arthurian Legends. (n.d.). *12th-century texts compiled from Geoffrey of Monmouth, Chrétien de Troyes, and Thomas Malory.* Bodleian Library.

Ayto, J. (2010). *Oxford dictionary of English idioms.* Oxford University Press.

Babbel Magazine. (2024, August 15). A guide to the many, many sports idioms of English. Retrieved March 4, 2025, from https://www.babbel.com/en/magazine/english-sports-idioms

Bartlett, R. (1986). *Trial by Fire and Water: The Medieval Judicial Ordeal.* Oxford University Press.

Baseball Almanac. (n.d.). Out in left field. In *Baseball Dictionary.* Retrieved March 4, 2025, from https://www.baseball-almanac.com/dictionary-term.php?term=out+in+left+field

Baum, L. F. (1900). *The wonderful wizard of Oz.* George M. Hill Company.

Benchley, P. (1974). *Jaws.* Doubleday.

Boston Consulting Group. (1968). *Research on corporate strategy, cash cows, and business growth models.* BCG Global Business Strategy Division.

Botanical Studies on Plant Temperature Regulation. (n.d.). *Research conducted by The Royal Botanic Gardens, Kew, and Harvard University's Plant Science Division.*

Bowen, T. (2005, June 1). Phrase of the week: A dark horse. *Onestopenglish.* Retrieved March 4, 2025, from https://www.onestopenglish.com/your-english/phrase-of-the-week-a-dark-horse/154188.article

Brewer, E. C. (1898). *Dictionary of phrase and fable.* Cassell & Company.

British Medieval History Archives. (n.d.). *Collection of legal records, manuscripts, and daily life accounts (1100s-1500s).* British Library and National Archives UK.

Burns, R. (1785). To a mouse. John Wilson.

Cambridge Dictionary. (n.d.). *Like a cat on a hot tin roof.* In *Cambridge Advanced Learner's Dictionary & Thesaurus.*

Cambridge University Press. (n.d.-a). Back to the drawing board. In *Cambridge Dictionary.* Retrieved March 4, 2025, from https://dictionary.cambridge.org/us/dictionary/english/back-to-the-drawing-board

Cambridge University Press. (n.d.-b). Off to a running start. In *Cambridge English Dictionary.* Retrieved March 4, 2025, from https://dictionary.cambridge.org/dictionary/english/off-to-a-running-start

Cambridge University Press. (n.d.-c). Play hardball. In *Cambridge English Dictionary.* Retrieved March 4, 2025, from https://dictionary.cambridge.org/us/dictionary/english/play-hardball

Cambridge University Press. (n.d.-d). Run interference. In *Cambridge English Dictionary.* Retrieved March 4, 2025, from https://dictionary.cambridge.org/us/dictionary/english/run-interference

Cambridge University Press. (n.d.-e). Take one for the team. In *Cambridge Dictionary.* Retrieved March 4, 2025, from https://dictionary.cambridge.org/us/dictionary/english/take-one-for-the-team

Casino & Gambling History Archives. (n.d.). *Studies on gambling culture, casino scandals, and betting strategies.* Nevada State Museum & The Las Vegas Mob Museum.

Chaucer, G. (1971). *Troilus and Criseyde* (N. Coghill, Trans.). Penguin Classics. (Original work published c. 1380)

Chaucer, G. (2005). *The Canterbury tales* (J. Mann, Ed.). Penguin Classics. (Original work published c. 1390)

Chekhov, A. (1997). *Five plays* (R. Hingley, Trans.). Oxford University Press. (Original work published 1889)

Christie, A. (1934). *Murder on the Orient Express.* Collins Crime Club.

Cicero. (1999). *Letters to Atticus* (D. R. Shackleton Bailey, Trans.). Harvard University Press. (Original work published 1st century BC)

Cobbett, W. (1807). *Weekly political register.* C. Clement.

Cohen, M. N. (1995). *Lewis Carroll: A biography.* Alfred A. Knopf.

Dallow, A. (Director). (2006, April 5). Like a bull in a china shop [Television series episode]. In *MythBusters.* Discovery Channel.

Darnton, R. (1996). *The great cat massacre and other episodes in French cultural history.* Basic Books.

Dictionary.com. (n.d.-a). On thin ice. Retrieved March 4, 2025, from https://www.dictionary.com/browse/on-thin-ice

Dictionary.com. (n.d.-b). Run interference. In *The American Heritage® Idioms Dictionary.* Retrieved March 4, 2025, from https://www.dictionary.com/browse/run-interference

Doyle, A. C. (1887-1927). *Sherlock Holmes series*. Harper & Brothers.

Dowson, E. (1894). Non sum qualis eram bonae sub regno cynarae. The Bodley Head.

EDS. (2000). *Cat herders* [Television commercial]. Super Bowl XXXIV.

Etymonline. (n.d.). Head over heels. Retrieved March 4, 2025, from https://www. etymonline.com/word/head%20over%20heels

Financial Times. (2025, February 15). *The Midas touch: 4,000 years of getting it wrong about gold*. Retrieved from https://www.ft.com/content/16d13b98-b1e7-4454-87c9-6f9060723f58

Fitzherbert, J. (1534). *The boke of husbandry*. Thomas Berthelet.

Fleming, V. (Director). (1939). *The wizard of Oz* [Film]. Metro-Goldwyn-Mayer.

Franklin, B. (1733-1758). *Poor Richard's almanack*. Self-published.

Franklin, B. (1748). *Advice to a young tradesman*. Self-published.

Funny Girl. (1964). [Film]. Columbia Pictures.

Gay, J. (1732). *Poems on several occasions*. J. Tonson & J. Watts.

Gerrold, D. (2001). *The world of Star Trek*. BenBella Books.

Ginger Software. (n.d.). Jump the gun | phrase definition, origin & examples. Retrieved March 4, 2025, from https://www.gingersoftware.com/content/ phrases/jump-the-gun

Grammar Monster. (n.d.-a). "Back to the drawing board". Retrieved March 4, 2025, from https://www.grammar-monster.com/sayings_proverbs/back_to_the_ drawing_board.htm

Grammar Monster. (n.d.-b). "Hanging by a thread" | Origin and meaning. Retrieved March 4, 2025, from https://www.grammar-monster.com/sayings_proverbs/ hanging_by_a_thread.htm

Grammar Monster. (n.d.-c). "Saved by the bell" | origin and meaning. Retrieved March 4, 2025, from https://www.grammar-monster.com/sayings_proverbs/ saved_by_the_bell.htm

Grammarist. (n.d.-a). Cover all the bases. Retrieved March 4, 2025, from https:// grammarist.com/usage/cover-all-the-bases/

Grammarist. (n.d.-b). Full-court press – idiom, meaning and origin. Retrieved March 4, 2025, from https://grammarist.com/idiom/full-court-press/

Grammarist. (n.d.-c). Jump the gun – idiom, origin & meaning. Retrieved March 4, 2025, from https://grammarist.com/idiom/jump-the-gun/

Grammarist. (n.d.-d). Neck and neck: Meaning and examples. Retrieved March 4, 2025, from https://grammarist.com/usage/neck-and-neck/

Grammarist. (n.d.-e). On the ropes – expressing helplessness or instigating fight back. Retrieved March 4, 2025, from https://grammarist.com/idiom/on-the-ropes/

Grammarist. (n.d.-f). Out of left field – meaning and origin. Retrieved March 4, 2025, from https://grammarist.com/idiom/out-of-left-field/

Grammarist. (n.d.-g). Play hardball. Retrieved March 4, 2025, from https://grammarist.com/idiom/play-hardball/

Grammarist. (n.d.-h). Step up to the plate – assuming the challenge. Retrieved March 4, 2025, from https://grammarist.com/idiom/step-up-to-the-plate/

Grammarist. (n.d.-i). Throw a curveball and throw a curve. Retrieved March 4, 2025, from https://grammarist.com/idiom/throw-a-curveball-and-throw-a-curve/

Grammarist. (n.d.-j). Throw in the towel; The ball is in your court; Move the goalposts. Retrieved March 4, 2025, from https://grammarist.com/idiom/throw-in-the-towel/

Grammarist. (n.d.-k). Throw your hat in the ring – idiom, meaning and origin. Retrieved March 4, 2025, from https://grammarist.com/idiom/throw-your-hat-in-the-ring/

Grammarist. (n.d.). *Trial by fire—Idiom, meaning & origin*. Retrieved March 10, 2025, from https://grammarist.com/idiom/trial-by-fire/

Green, J. (2010). *Green's Dictionary of Slang* (Vol. 2). Chambers.

Green, J. (2011). *Green's dictionary of slang*. Oxford University Press.

Gutoskey, E. (2022, August 26). *Why does having 'egg on your face' mean you're embarrassed?* Mental Floss.

Haining, P. (1981). *The classic era of crime fiction*. Dover Publications.

Heller, J. (1961). *Catch-22*. Simon & Schuster.

Hesiod. (1988). *Works and days* (M. L. West, Trans.). Oxford University Press. (Original work published 8th century BC)

Heywood, J. (1546). *A Dialogue Containing the Number in Effect of All the Proverbs in the English Tongue*. Thomas Berthelet.

Hislop, A. (1862). *Scottish national proverbs & sayings*. William P. Nimmo.

Homer. (1990). *The Iliad* (R. Fagles, Trans.). Penguin Classics. (Original work published 8th century BC)

Horse Racing History Archives. (n.d.). *Records of Thoroughbred Racing & Betting Trends (1600s-Present)*. National Museum of Racing and Hall of Fame.

Howell, J. (1659). *Proverbs*. Henry Herringman.

Idioms Online. (n.d.). Run interference. Retrieved March 4, 2025, from https://www.idioms.online/run-interference/

International Cloud Atlas. (1896). World Meteorological Organization.

Irish Folklore Archives. (n.d.). *Compiled oral traditions, myths, and legends*. National Folklore Collection, University College Dublin.

It's the bee's knees; or, the entomology and etymology of 'The Bee's Knees'. (2022,

June 6). In The Marietta Traveler. Retrieved from https://www.mariettatraveler.com/bees-knees-etymology

The bee's knees. (n.d.). In Wiktionary. Retrieved from https://en.wiktionary.org/wiki/bee%27s_knees

Jackson, K. (2007). *Classics of the horror film*. Citadel Press.

Kennedy, J. F. (1963, October). *Economic policy speech* [Speech transcript]. John F. Kennedy Presidential Library and Museum.

Know Your Phrase. (n.d.-a). On the ropes – meaning and origin. Retrieved March 4, 2025, from https://knowyourphrase.com/on-the-ropes

Know Your Phrase. (n.d.-b). The ball is in your court – meaning and origin; Move the goalposts – meaning and origin. Retrieved March 4, 2025, from https://knowyourphrase.com/the-ball-is-in-your-court

LanGeek. (n.d.-a). Definition & meaning of "on the ropes". Retrieved March 4, 2025, from https://dictionary.langeek.co/en/word/212383

LanGeek. (n.d.-b). Definition & meaning of "throw a curveball". Retrieved March 4, 2025, from https://dictionary.langeek.co/en/word/214229

LanGeek. (n.d.-c). Jump the gun. Retrieved March 4, 2025, from https://dictionary.langeek.co/en/word/213537

Lawrence, H. (1771). *Contemplative Man* (p. 78). T. Cadell.

Lucas, G. (Director). (1977). *Star wars: A new hope* [Film]. 20th Century Fox.

Lyly, J. (1580). *Euphues and his England*. Thomas East.

Macmillan, H. (1960, February 3). *The wind of change* [Speech transcript]. UK National Archives.

Martin, G. (2023, December 11). A dark horse. The Phrase Finder. Retrieved March 4, 2025, from https://www.phrases.org.uk/meanings/dark-horse.html

McGill Office for Science and Society. (2023). Saved by the bell. Retrieved March 4, 2025, from https://www.mcgill.ca/oss/article/history-did-you-know/saved-bell

Melville, H. (1851). *Moby-Dick*. Harper & Brothers.

Merriam-Webster. (n.d.-a). Bat a thousand. Retrieved March 4, 2025, from https://www.merriam-webster.com/dictionary/bat%20a%20thousand

Merriam-Webster. (n.d.-b). Full-court press. Retrieved March 4, 2025, from https://www.merriam-webster.com/dictionary/full-court%20press

Merriam-Webster. (n.d.-c). Get/start off to a running start. Retrieved March 4, 2025, from https://www.merriam-webster.com/dictionary/get%2Fstart%20off%20to%20a%20running%20start

Merriam-Webster. (n.d.-d). Hang by a thread. Retrieved March 4, 2025, from https://www.merriam-webster.com/dictionary/hang%20by%20a%20thread

Merriam-Webster. (n.d.-e). Neck and neck. Retrieved March 4, 2025, from https://www.merriam-webster.com/dictionary/neck%20and%20neck

Merriam-Webster. (n.d.-f). Step up to the plate. Retrieved March 4, 2025, from https://www.merriam-webster.com/dictionary/step%20up%20to%20the%20plate

Merriam-Webster. (n.d.-g). Tee up. Retrieved March 4, 2025, from https://www.merriam-webster.com/dictionary/tee%20up

Merriam-Webster. (n.d.-h). Throw (someone) a curve/curveball. Retrieved March 4, 2025, from https://www.merriam-webster.com/dictionary/throw%20%28someone%29%20a%20curve%2Fcurveball

Milton, J. (1634). *Comus*. Humphrey Moseley.

Mitchell, M. (1936). *Gone with the wind*. Macmillan.

Momand, A. R. (1913). Keeping up with the Joneses. *New York World*.

National Hurricane Center Archives. (n.d.). *Compiled data on tropical storms and hurricanes*. National Oceanic and Atmospheric Administration.

National Oceanic and Atmospheric Administration. (1950-present). *Meteorological and climate research reports*. www.noaa.gov

National Weather Service Archives. (n.d.). *Historical meteorological data*. U.S. National Weather Service and National Climatic Data Center.

Naval & Military History Archives. (n.d.). *Research compiled from The National Museum of the Royal Navy, The U.S. Naval Institute, and West Point Military Academy*.

Neuroscience & Animal Behavior Studies. (2000-2022). *Research compiled by Harvard Medical School and Cornell University Veterinary College*.

New Advent. (n.d.). *Ordeal by fire*. Retrieved March 10, 2025, from https://www.newadvent.org/cathen/11276b.htm

North, T. (1579). *Plutarch's lives*. Richard Field.

Online Etymology Dictionary. (n.d.). (D. Harper, Ed.). www.etymonline.com

Orwell, G. (1949). *1984*. Secker & Warburg.

Overbury, T. (1613). *A wife*. Thomas Creede.

Ovid. (n.d.). *Metamorphoses XI*. In *Theoi Classical Texts Library*. Retrieved from https://www.theoi.com/Text/OvidMetamorphoses11.html

Oxford English Dictionary. (n.d.-a). A bitter pill to swallow; Blood is thicker than water; Eat humble pie; Hair's breadth; Head over heels; Out of the frying pan into the fire; Rub salt in the wound. Retrieved March 4, 2025, from https://www.oed.com

Oxford English Dictionary. (n.d.-b). On the ropes. Oxford University Press.

Oxford English Dictionary. (n.d.-c). Saved by the bell. Oxford University Press.

Oxford English Dictionary. (n.d.-d). Throw in the towel. Oxford University Press.

Partridge, E. (1985). *A Dictionary of Catch Phrases: British and American, from the Sixteenth Century to the Present Day*. Routledge.

Perrault, C. (1697). *Cendrillon, ou la petite pantoufle de verre*. Claude Barbin.

Phrase Finder. (n.d.). Head over heels. Retrieved March 4, 2025, from https://www.phrases.org.uk/meanings/head-over-heels.html

Phrases.org.uk. (n.d.). Saved by the bell – meaning & origin of the phrase. Retrieved March 4, 2025, from https://www.phrases.org.uk/meanings/saved-by-the-bell.html

Pliny the Elder. (1938). *Natural history* (H. Rackham, Trans.). Harvard University Press. (Original work published 77 AD)

Porter, L. (2015). *Watching television: A history of American television*. Routledge.

Quarles, F. (1635). *Emblemes*. John Marriott.

Quinion, M. (2009). *Egg on one's face*. World Wide Words.

Ray, J. (1670). *A Collection of English Proverbs*. Cambridge University Press.

Rinehart, M. R. (1930). *The door*. Farrar & Rinehart.

Roste, R. (n.d.). Skating on thin ice. In *Grammar Stuff - The Writing Life*. Retrieved March 4, 2025, from https://robynroste.com/skating-on-thin-ice/

Rousseau, J. J. (1765). *Confessions*. Marc-Michel Rey.

Royal Navy Historical Archives. (n.d.). *Documents detailing naval strategy, battles, and shipbuilding from the 16th century to modern times*. National Museum of the Royal Navy.

Safire, W. (2008). *Safire's political dictionary*. Oxford University Press.

Scorsese, M. (Director). (2013). *The wolf of Wall Street* [Film]. Paramount Pictures.

Scott, W. (1816). *The antiquary*. Archibald Constable.

Seinfeld. (1997). The yada yada (Season 8, Episode 19) [TV series episode]. NBC Television.

Shakespeare, W. (1984). *Romeo and Juliet* (G. B. Evans, Ed.). Cambridge University Press. (Original work published 1595)

Shakespeare, W. (1997). *Othello* (E. A. J. Honigmann, Ed.). Arden Shakespeare. (Original work published 1604)

Shakespeare, W. (1998). *Julius Caesar* (D. Daniell, Ed.). Arden Shakespeare. (Original work published 1599)

Shakespeare, W. (2002). *King Henry IV, Part 1* (D. S. Kastan, Ed.). Arden Shakespeare. (Original work published 1597)

Shakespeare, W. (2005a). *King John* (A. R. Braunmuller, Ed.). Arden Shakespeare. (Original work published 1597)

Shakespeare, W. (2005b). *The tempest* (F. Kermode, Ed.). Cambridge University Press. (Original work published 1611)

Shakespeare, W. (2008). *Hamlet* (G. R. Hibbard, Ed.). Oxford University Press. (Original work published 1603)

Shatner, W., & Kreski, C. (1993). *Star Trek memories*. HarperCollins.

Spears, R. A. (2005). *McGraw-Hill's dictionary of American idioms and phrasal verbs*. McGraw-Hill.

Spenser, E. (1590). *The Faerie Queene*. William Ponsonby.

Steinbeck, J. (1937). *Of mice and men*. Covici-Friede.

Stevenson, R. L. (1886). *Strange case of Dr. Jekyll and Mr. Hyde*. Longmans, Green & Co.

Swift, J. (1738). *A complete collection of polite and ingenious conversation*. Charles Bathurst.

Symons, J. (1992). *Bloody murder: From the detective story to the crime novel*. Penguin Books.

Taylor, C. (2013). *The Unauthorized Star Wars Story: David Prowse, Darth Vader, and the Hidden Feud*. Film History Press.

Team Tactics. (2024, June 15). Taking one for the team: Meaning & origins. Retrieved March 4, 2025, from https://www.teamtactics.co.uk/blog/taking-one-for-the-team/

The Bible. King James Version. (1611). www.biblegateway.com

The Free Dictionary. (n.d.). Off to a running start. Retrieved March 4, 2025, from https://idioms.thefreedictionary.com/off+to+a+running+start

The Idioms. (n.d.-a). Down to the wire. Retrieved March 4, 2025, from https://www.theidioms.com/down-to-the-wire/

The Idioms. (n.d.-b). Hang by a thread. Retrieved March 4, 2025, from https://www.theidioms.com/hang-by-a-thread/

The Idioms. (n.d.). *Like a cat on a hot tin roof.*

The Idioms. (n.d.-c). Neck and neck: Meaning, origin, example, sentence, history. Retrieved March 4, 2025, from https://www.theidioms.com/neck-and-neck/

The Idioms. (n.d.-d). Skating on thin ice: Meaning, origin, example, sentence, history. Retrieved March 4, 2025, from https://www.theidioms.com/skating-on-thin-ice/

The Idioms. (n.d.-e). Throw in the towel; The ball is in your court; Move the goalposts. Retrieved March 4, 2025, from https://www.theidioms.com/throw-in-the-towel/

The Idioms. (n.d.-f). Throw your hat in the ring. Retrieved March 4, 2025, from https://www.theidioms.com/throw-your-hat-in-the-ring/

The Lebanon Patriot. (1833). Lotta's Romantic Tale (p. 4). Indiana Historical Archives.

The Phrase Finder. (n.d.-a). Down to the wire. Retrieved March 4, 2025, from https://www.phrases.org.uk/meanings/down-to-the-wire.html

The Phrase Finder. (n.d.-b). Step up to the plate. Retrieved March 4, 2025, from https://www.phrases.org.uk/meanings/step-up-to-the-plate.html

The Phrase Finder. (n.d.-c). Throw your hat in the ring. Retrieved March 4, 2025, from https://www.phrases.org.uk/meanings/throw-your-hat-in-the-ring.html

The Sun. (2024, November 27). *Mystery message carved into statue forged by King*

Midas is read for FIRST time in 2,600yrs after one-in-a-million photo. Retrieved from https://www.thesun.co.uk/tech/31958640/mystery-message-statue-king-midas/

The TR Company. (2019, April 15). Cover all the bases. Retrieved March 4, 2025, from https://thetrcompany.com/en/cover-all-the-bases/

Tolkien, J. R. R. (1955). *The return of the king.* Allen & Unwin.

Truitt, B. (2015). The cinema of coincidence: Deus ex machina in modern story-telling. *Film Studies Journal, 18*(2), 37-54.

Truman, H. S. (1953). *Public Papers of the Presidents of the United States: Harry S. Truman.* U.S. Government Printing Office.

Turan, K. (2005). *Never coming to a theater near you: A celebration of a certain kind of movie.* PublicAffairs.

Twain, M. (1888). *Letter to William Dean Howells.*

Tyndale, W. (1526). *The New Testament.* Peter Schoeffer.

U.S. Civil War Telegraph Records. (n.d.). *Digitized documents on military communication, coded messages, and telegraph strategies.* Library of Congress and The National Civil War Museum.

Vogler, C. (2007). *The writer's journey: Mythic structure for writers* (3rd ed.). Michael Wiese Productions.

Warhol, A. (1968). *Art and mass media commentary.* Random House.

Wikipedia contributors. (2025, January 15). *Cat on a Hot Tin Roof.* In *Wikipedia, The Free Encyclopedia.* Retrieved from

Wikipedia contributors. (2025, January 20). *Don't throw the baby out with the bathwater.* In *Wikipedia, The Free Encyclopedia.* Retrieved from

Wikipedia contributors. (2024, September 15). Full-court press. In *Wikipedia, The Free Encyclopedia.* Retrieved March 4, 2025, from https://en.wikipedia.org/wiki/Full-court_press

Wikipedia contributors. (2025a, January 3). Out of left field. In *Wikipedia, The Free Encyclopedia.* Retrieved March 4, 2025, from https://en.wikipedia.org/wiki/Out_of_left_field

Wikipedia contributors. (2025b, March 3). Glossary of English-language idioms derived from baseball. In *Wikipedia, The Free Encyclopedia.* Retrieved March 4, 2025, from https://en.wikipedia.org/wiki/Glossary_of_English-language_idioms_derived_from_baseball

Wikipedia contributors. (2025, March 1). *Midas.* In *Wikipedia, The Free Encyclopedia.* Retrieved from https://en.wikipedia.org/wiki/Midas

Wikipedia contributors. (2025, March 10). *Trial by ordeal.* In *Wikipedia, The Free Encyclopedia.* Retrieved from https://en.wikipedia.org/wiki/Trial_by_ordeal

Wiktionary. (n.d.-a). Bat a thousand. Retrieved March 4, 2025, from https://en.wiktionary.org/wiki/bat_a_thousand

Wiktionary. (n.d.-b). Head over heels. Retrieved March 4, 2025, from https://en.
wiktionary.org/wiki/head_over_heels

Wiktionary. (n.d.-c). Play hardball. Retrieved March 4, 2025, from https://en.wik
tionary.org/wiki/play_hardball

Wiktionary. (n.d.-d). Take one for the team. Retrieved March 4, 2025, from https://
en.wiktionary.org/wiki/take_one_for_the_team

Wiktionary. (n.d.-e). Tee up. Retrieved March 4, 2025, from https://en.wiktionary.
org/wiki/tee_up

Wiktionary. (n.d.). *Trial by fire*. Retrieved March 10, 2025, from https://en.wik
tionary.org/wiki/trial_by_fire

Wilde, O. (1890). *The picture of Dorian Gray*. Ward, Lock & Co.

Wilton, D. (2004). *Word Myths: Debunking Linguistic Urban Legends*. Oxford
University Press.

Withals, J. (1616). *A short dictionary for young beginners*. Richard Tottell.

Zoological Studies on Bees & Pollination. (1980-Present). *Research from the
Smithsonian Institution & University of Cambridge*.

Zuckerman, E. (2011). *Jaws: The making of a Hollywood classic*. HarperCollins.

www.ingramcontent.com/pod-product-compliance
Lightning Source LLC
Chambersburg PA
CBHW071526120626
46550CB00006B/2371